# BLACK
## IN BLUE

# CARMEN BEST

# BLACK IN BLUE

## LESSONS ON LEADERSHIP, BREAKING BARRIERS, AND RACIAL RECONCILIATION

HarperCollins
Leadership

An Imprint of HarperCollins

Published by HarperCollins Leadership, an imprint of HarperCollins Focus LLC.

Any internet addresses, phone numbers, or company or product information printed in this book are offered as a resource and are not intended in any way to be or to imply an endorsement by HarperCollins Leadership, nor does HarperCollins Leadership vouch for the existence, content, or services of these sites, phone numbers, companies, or products beyond the life of this book.

ISBN 978-1-4002-3062-4 (eBook)
ISBN 978-1-4002-3061-7 (HC)

**Library of Congress Cataloging-in-Publication Data**
Library of Congress Cataloging-in-Publication application has been submitted.

Printed in the United States of America
21 22 23 24 25  LSC  10 9 8 7 6 5 4 3 2 1

To my daughters and grandchild,
for their constant support and unconditional love.

# CONTENTS

# ACKNOWLEDGMENTS

**THIS BOOK WOULD** not have been possible without the help, support, and inspiration of the following people. First and foremost, my daughters, who have always been sources of strength and perseverance for me, who stood by me and motivated me to power through and never give up, no matter the challenge. This book would not exist without you, and for that and many other reasons, I will always be thankful to you. To my grandchild, who brings so much love and sunshine to my life. It was knowing that one day you will read this book and get to know me a little bit better through my words that pushed me to keep writing.

To my lawyers, Robert Barnett, who guided me through the unknowns of the publishing industry, and Anne Bremner, who gave legal advice and guidance the way only a true friend could. To Sara Kendrick at HarperCollins Leadership, for seeing my vision for the book and embracing it. To Chris Fisher, who helped quietly behind the scenes and kept me focused. To Brunella

## ACKNOWLEDGMENTS

Costagliola at Kevin Anderson & Associates, for your help, time, and dedication: this book would not have happened without you.

To my many mentors, allies, and sponsors, who have supported me along the way, who believed in me, who opened doors for me, who pulled out a chair so I could have the proverbial seat at the table.

To my community, for allowing me to serve you. To my fellow African Americans, for being sources of great pride to me. To the countless men and women in uniform, who choose to serve their country and keep it safe every single day.

And, last but not least, to you, for taking the time to read this book, which above all else has been a true labor of love. I hope you find it inspiring and encouraging.

Yours truly,
Carmen Best

# INTRODUCTION

**LET'S HAVE AN** honest conversation, shall we? Police brutality is real. Racism is real. Sexism is real. These are truths that simply cannot be denied. We read about them every day in the newspapers, we see them on television, and we witness them in our neighborhoods, as more and more stories of African American men and women whose lives are stolen by White police officers saturate our brains and crush our hearts.

I have served in the Seattle police force for almost thirty years, and the last almost three years of my career I was appointed chief of police, the first Black woman to ever hold that role in Seattle. And believe me when I tell you that, as a woman working in a male-dominated field and a Black Lives Matter supporter employed by the police force, I have experienced firsthand how excruciatingly present—and just how deeply rooted—racism and sexism are in every aspect of society, and yes that includes policing.

I started my career the same year that police officers assaulted Rodney King in Los Angeles, and I retired the same year that police officers killed George Floyd and Breonna Taylor—just to name two of the 164 African Americans killed by the police in the first eight months of 2020. These were the same killings that in June 2020 prompted the Capitol Hill Autonomous Zone (CHAZ) in Seattle, which soon escalated to the Capitol Hill Occupied Protest (CHOP), where people occupied the East Precinct and the streets while carrying weapons and inciting the crowds with signs that read "Who prosecutes the police?" "Black Lives Matter!" "Defund the police!" "Abolish SPD!" The day before my retirement, after witnessing so much pain in my community, I remember thinking to myself: *How is it that we are still facing the same issues we faced almost thirty years ago when I began my career in policing?* I carried a badge and a gun for nearly three decades and my only goal was to make things better. Did I accomplish that?

As chief, I led a group of officers that better mirrored the cultural diversity that characterizes our country—reaching record-breaking diversity hiring and recruitment within the department. I strived to engage with my community to ensure public safety, gender equity, and inclusion. I applauded and supported officers who positively influenced the community, and I fired those whose morals, values, and codes of conduct to me smacked of racism and sexism, thus going against the core principles of policing—those officers who, fueled by their poisonous prejudices, served apart from the community instead of serving as part of the community.

Yet, while much has changed, it hasn't been nearly enough, and these pervasive problems still exist. More violent riots erupted, more people demanded to defund the police, and more Black mothers and fathers mourned the loss of their children. And I found myself in the middle of it all, as a Black woman and mother but also the chief of police and defender of the US Constitution, as a believer in law and order as well as in the Black Lives Matter movement. To many, it seemed like the two versions of me couldn't peacefully coexist in our society. To me, it was a no-brainer: Why *wouldn't* I want to be part of the police force? After all, I am a clear representation of what the police force as a whole is: a big dichotomy. But the scale is unbalanced, and I think you would be surprised to learn that, in my opinion, the side weighing more than the other is the positive one.

Over the years, I have witnessed my fellow officers make more of a positive impact in our community and society than a negative one. I have led more officers who cared deeply about their fellow citizens than those who didn't. I have seen change take place—although not as quickly as we would hope or need—within the police force, such as when my predecessor, a woman, appointed me to be her deputy chief, thus paving the way for me to then one day become the first Black female chief in Seattle.

Racist, sexist, bad people are everywhere in this country, and they work in every profession. Yet stories of police brutality claim the front pages of the country's newspapers because police officers have the power to take away people's freedom. They can put people in handcuffs and take them to jail. They can shoot them and harm them—and, under certain circumstances, they do so justifiably. But racism doesn't start and end with the police force. Racism exists everywhere: in education, health care, and every other industry. And that's why I am a firm believer that defunding the police is not the answer, because the police force is not the crux of the problem. There is a culturally pervasive and inherent malignancy that manifests itself in almost every aspect of society.

So what can we do to bring forth the change our society so desperately needs? First and foremost, we must acknowledge history. And history tells us that the police force has often been on the wrong side of history, and there's no way we can make things better unless we are willing to accept the truth of this statement. The police force hasn't always supported the Black community, the Asian community, the Latino community, the LGBTQ+ community, the poor White community, and the many other minorities that enrich our country but have been marginalized for too long.

Once we finally acknowledge history, we can find ways to avoid repeating the same mistakes. It is my core belief that mistakes don't start in the actual profession but much earlier, even before a man or woman chooses to become a police officer or a teacher or a doctor or a social worker. It starts at home, and it starts during childhood. Some of the most important leadership principles that I applied throughout my life, especially as chief of police, I learned as a child at home, in school, and among my peers.

And this is what I will be sharing with you in my book: leadership lessons that have helped me not only in my career but also in life, as well as behind-the-scenes accounts on CHAZ, CHOP, and what really happened when my name did not make the list of the top three candidates for the coveted position of chief of police. I will share values and principles that I stood by even when I knew the decisions I made as chief were not going to be well received by the court of public opinion, decisions I stood by because I knew it was the right thing to do.

After all, leading a group of people, an organization, a company, a community means placing your own personal views aside and doing what is lawful and right. And *that* is the hardest lesson to learn.

# PROLOGUE

**THE SEATTLE WIND,** uncharacteristically cold for late spring, greeted me the moment I stepped outside police headquarters, sending a quick chill down my spine and reminding me that I had completely forgotten to put my coat on.

Oh well.

I blamed my unusual absentmindedness on the fact that, during the call, Mayor Jenny Durkan sounded rather cryptic when she said she needed to see me as soon as possible.

As I walked across the street to city hall, I felt my heart rate go up and a surge of energy rush through my body. I began speeding up as if pushed by an invisible motivational force, the kind you get when you know that this is an important day in your life and you're about to receive that good news you've been waiting for.

The faster I walked, the harder the wind hit my face. Yet, for some reason, my skin didn't feel the piercing chill that the Pacific Northwest wind is known for. It was almost as if that same invisible force had created a shield around me, protecting me against the elements.

Once inside the building, I walked at a quick pace toward the elevator.

"Good morning, Chief Best," I heard twice in the distance but didn't turn to look at who it was. Instead, I kept my eyes focused on that elevator and simply waved in response.

When the elevator doors opened, I stepped inside and quickly pressed the button that would take me to the mayor's office, on the seventh floor.

*Man, does it always take so long?* I thought to myself as I stared at the floor numbers slowly changing on the monitor.

Three . . . four . . .

I crossed my arms and kept staring.

Five . . . six . . .

I began tapping with my right foot.

Seven!

I let out a deep sigh and closed my eyes to collect myself before the doors opened.

I walked out of the elevator and headed for her office. Then I knocked on the door—which was slightly open— and waited for my cue.

"Please come in."

*There it is.*

I walked in and offered her a smile. She was sitting behind her conference table, her blonde hair nicely done in her signature longer bob haircut, and dressed elegantly, as always.

"Chief Best," she said. "Please sit down."

I followed her invite and sat down in front of her, my open palms resting on my lap.

This was it. The moment I had been waiting for since Chief Kathleen O'Toole had stepped down as chief of police and Mayor Durkan appointed me interim chief. The whole community had been buzzing about me becoming chief—and, as much as I tried, it was hard to ignore the rumors, because it meant that people in my community appreciated how much I cared for them and just how hard I worked to ensure their safety. I had been part of the police force since 1992, and if there was one thing I was certain of, it was that I always strove to serve my community. I had so many plans and ideas on how to improve community and police interactions, and I couldn't wait to get started. I knew the city better than the palm of my hand. I walked every neighborhood, was aware of every safety issue our community faced, and had already been leading fourteen hundred officers for five months now as the interim chief. I knew I was one of the semifinalists and had been waiting to hear that I had made the top three.

I took a deep breath, ready to hear the good news with a smile on my face.

Mayor Durkan looked at me, then down at her conference table as if to avoid making eye contact. This sent shivers down my body, but before I could read her body language even more, she spoke.

"You didn't make the top three."

*What?*

The invisible force disappeared. The shield disintegrated. The words hit me right in the chest.

*What?*

My arms fell to the side.

"I know it must be so . . ." She was talking. I was staring at her, but I didn't see her. Nor did I hear her.

"I know how you feel"—her words echoed in the room that suddenly felt empty and cold—"it reminds me of that time I was overlooked"—*what the*, I stared at her—"for a promotion at the Department of Justice."

I couldn't believe she was talking about herself. In that very moment.

*What the hell does that have to do with me and my situation?*

I wanted to scream at her but chose not to voice the thought and left it silent within me. She stopped talking and just looked at me. Her expression and my disappointment brought tears to my eyes, shocking me out of my muted conversation and forcing me to keep my composure.

She and I—and everybody else, for that matter—knew that I was the most qualified one on that list. I had the most education, training, and experience required to be chief of police. Period. I had already put in so much work as the interim, not to mention the decades I had dedicated to the department, the community, the city.

"Oh," I said, clearing my voice. "Well, I don't think this was a fair process. If it were, I would have ended up in the top three."

I got up, walked out of her office, and heard them: there was a press conference happening right in the room next to her office, announcing to the media and the public the top three candidates for the position of chief of police.

I had to get out of there before anybody saw me and asked me for a statement. I hadn't had any time to process what had just happened. Something had gone wrong within this selection process, and the results just didn't make any sense. I decided to walk down the back stairs, foregoing the elevator to avoid coming across the media; so I left the building through the back way.

"Mom, what's going on?" my daughter wrote me in a text message.

*She must be watching the live broadcast,* I thought as the cold spring air scraped painful trenches down my cheeks. My eyes burning with tears not allowed to be.

I entered the police headquarters and took the elevator up to my office. The doors opened and standing right there in the hall of the eighth floor were about a dozen colleagues, their open-wide eyes and parted lips conveying their shock and disappointment, their crossed arms a sign of their frustration and anger. I could hear "What?" "How in the world?" and other expressions that voiced their disbelief.

No time to waste; I knew they needed to hear from me. I couldn't afford the luxury of taking time to process what had just happened on a personal level. No, they needed me to be the leader I had always been. And I knew what I had to do: share what I knew of the situation, acknowledge their feelings, and remind them of the importance of moving forward, as a team. So I stepped toward them, looked at them, and said: "Listen, I don't know what happened exactly. I see you are disappointed and understand why, but we still have to focus on our jobs, our community, and our responsibilities. So come on, let's get back to work."

Then, I went back to my office, closed the door, sat down at my desk, placed my open palms on my lap, and looked at a pile of papers I had just gone through that morning, a pile that represented the proverbial tip of the iceberg of what my officers and I had accomplished so far. And yet none of it had been taken into account when choosing the top candidates. I wondered whether bias by the decision makers played a much bigger role than credentials, commitment, and proven ability.

Regardless, this was the situation my department and I had been dealt. So there was only one thing I could do: face it. I took a piece of paper and jotted down a draft of my statement to the Seattle police force:

There is no greater honor than to have served as the Chief of the Seattle Police Department, in a city and department that I love. I want to thank the Mayor for the opportunity and have agreed to her request that I continue as Interim Chief until a new Chief is confirmed. I wish the candidates the best—each of them should know how fortunate they will be to lead officers who have a commitment to public safety and reform. We will continue to work to meet our community's expectations, while leading the way as one of the best departments in the country, with Service, Pride, and Dedication.

Thank you.

I read it, felt satisfied with the content, and sent it out to my employees.

Time to get back to work.

# BLACK
## IN BLUE

# 1

# No Success
# Without Hard Work

There is no success without hard work. Period. And while it might seem obvious, this is the most difficult leadership principle to follow, because it requires a constant commitment to our goals and an unwavering belief in our values. Commitment feeds off of self-discipline, and self-discipline comes from a solid pattern of behavior that, I believe, is first and foremost acquired during childhood by paying attention to those around us who, leading by example, show us what to prioritize, how to overcome obstacles, and when to stand up for what we know is right.

It was indeed during my childhood that I witnessed what hard work looks like, and I strove to apply the lessons I learned within my household to my school years in order to achieve the success I desired. But let me tell you, it was no smooth road. I encountered many bumps along the way that almost convinced me to give up. But thankfully I had an inner drive—a natural consequence of the way I was raised—and people around me who supported me and helped me stay motivated and focused. I learned from every win and every failure. I gained experience from everything I conquered and everything I lost. But one thing I never did was give up, because I was raised not to be a quitter.

**I WAS BORN** in a lower-middle-class family. As a child, I didn't have much, but I did have two parents who instilled in me the foundations of hard work. While no one would say we lived in the lap of luxury—far from it—my parents amply provided for our needs. My father was in the US Army and often had to travel overseas for work for extended periods, leaving us behind. After he received orders to Fort Lewis—now Joint Base Lewis-McChord—near Tacoma, Washington, my parents bought a four-bedroom house that had a big backyard, where I enjoyed playing with my younger siblings and the neighborhood kids.

When my dad was home from missions, he drank a whole lot and was essentially a functioning alcoholic. I believe he loved us, but he was emotionally absent. He didn't help us with homework and didn't offer us advice. But you sure noticed when he was in the room as he loved to be the center of attention and had a great sense of humor. He also had a commanding presence, but he was not overbearing. That being said, he expected obedience from me and my siblings. He didn't speak often, but when he did, I listened. As a young girl, I often had anxiety because I worried my dad would lose his job due to his heavy drinking (that is, showing up late or with alcohol on his breath), and I knew that would have a detrimental effect on our entire family. Without his financial support, we would lose our home, and that was a real fear of mine.

My sweet and gentle mom was constantly busy. She worked as a nurse's aide at a nursing home at night and spent her days taking care of us, sleeping when she could to prepare for her night shift and later running an in-home day care that provided our family with a little extra money. Often parenting alone, she would send me or one of my siblings to the local tavern to deliver a message to my dad—no cell phones back then—or to bring my dad back home when she needed him to help her with something around the house.

She was also a good homemaker. I remember one time when my mother had just delivered my youngest brother—he was born on December 12—and my dad was still overseas in Germany. It was a freezing cold winter morning, with glistening ice on the road and the wind making the temperature feel about ten degrees lower than what the thermometer showed. I was almost five years old, and my brother and I were walking together to preschool. My mother, who had gone Christmas shopping for my brother and me after having the baby, had fallen ill and had been hospitalized with pneumonia. Although she was back home now and re-covering, she was under strict doctor's orders not to leave the house and to get as much rest as possible—eas-ier said than done, of course. Anyway, she knew it was going to be dangerously cold for us to walk to school, but we didn't have a choice. Still, she sewed us cloth mittens made out of leopard print material and sent us on our way.

Unfortunately, the cloth did not keep our hands warm. I felt so sorry for my little brother, his teeth chat-tering uncontrollably, that I gave him my mittens to wear. My fingers hurt for how cold they were. I tried putting my hands in my pockets, but they were just as cold. Blowing on them proved to be useless as well be-cause, although I was young, I knew that if I could *see* my breath, it meant it was too cold for it to warm up any-thing. Out of ideas, I glanced at my brother and saw that his chattering had been replaced by a shy smile. And that made it all worth it to me. I could deal with the cold, after all, as long as he was no longer shivering. To this day, this unabashed and pure moment of sibling love is one of my fondest childhood memories.

## Working Hard Is a Pattern of Behavior

My mom provided us with a stable—and strict—routine where our duties were clearly prioritized, no exceptions allowed: school and church came first, then family time and sports. And, of course, a little bit of extra time in the evening that we could dedicate to our hobbies. Mine was reading. I remember how comforting I found scooching into my bed, pulling the blanket over my head, turning the flashlight on to read when I was supposed to be fast asleep, and visiting wonderful worlds inhabited by magical creatures. Those were some of my favorite moments of the week.

Juxtaposed to that was going to church every Sunday. My mother would drag my siblings and me there, and we would spend hours upon hours praying and interacting with the church community. As a child, it was hard to see just how I could benefit from being forced to do something I found boring. But as an adult I realized just how much those Sundays affected me, shaped my view of the world, and kept me grounded. The positive impact they had on my values and core beliefs I held on tight to and fought for, even if it meant risking my entire career.

My mom came from a family of hardworking women, so it's no surprise that, throughout her whole life, my mom wore many different hats—adding college student to her list when I was in high school. But she also made sure we felt her love and presence, all the while setting for us an unwavering example of what sheer willpower and a sense of pride will help you accomplish in life. I know that the way she raised me and the example she set for me were major reasons why I never gave up during my high school years, no matter how many times I came face-to-face with defeat.

Like that one time I ran for student body president against two opponents. I wrote my speech with the goal of showing all the students that no matter how diverse we were, what cultural and religious background we came from, and what our future aspirations were, there was indeed one thing that unified us: our school.

"And so, it is important for us to believe in our abilities and to know that we can indeed make a difference," I repeated the night before I was due to make my speech. I was in my bedroom, side lamp on, pacing back and forth as I spoke to nobody.

"Knock knock," my mom said as she opened the door slightly. "May I come in?"

I nodded yes.

She stepped into the room, her arms behind her back, hiding something. I tried peeking.

"Uh-uh," she admonished me. "Not so fast. I made you something, but it's a surprise, so sit down."

I sat down on the edge of my bed, closed my eyes, and smiled. I didn't know what she had made for me, but whatever it was, in that moment I no longer felt like a teenager but more like I was five years old again and it was Christmas morning.

"All right." Her tone was gentle. "You can open your eyes now."

I did so slowly, and right in front of me was the most beautiful suit I had ever seen. My gasp filled with surprise betrayed the paced and controlled demeanor I had worked on to deliver my speech. A tan, tweed blazer and skirt. Simple and chic.

"You like it?" she asked, her eyebrows raised with anticipation.

"I love it, Mom!" I stood up and measured it against my body as I looked at myself in the mirror. "Thank you so much!"

"This way, you will not only sound truly professional tomorrow, but you'll look like a student body president as well." She tilted her head to look at my reflection.

It must have taken her hours to make the suit, and I had no idea where she had managed to find the time.

I moved slightly from side to side to see how the suit moved with me. It was amazing!

"Now, now. Stop admiring yourself and get back to rehearsing that speech. But don't forget to get some beauty sleep."

I thanked her, and she walked out of the room leaving the dress on my bed.

The next day, I drove to school and strode in tall and proud in my new suit. Holding a copy of my speech in my folder, I walked to the center of the gym where school officials had assembled a stand-up microphone. I took a deep breath, cleared my throat, and looked at my audience. At that moment, two of my girlfriends ran onto the gym floor hooting, chanting, and ringing a cow bell. They ran around the perimeter of the gym waving with a ten-foot-wide, three-foot-tall banner made from one of those huge construction paper rolls. The banner was decorated and read "Carmen for Student Body President." This was a complete surprise to me, and I felt a warm feeling of appreciation for their moral support and esprit de corps.

"My fellow students," I began, my tone measured and clear as I continued delivering my speech—which had gone through several drafts that included changes in vocabulary that would better convey my message of unity and school spirit—"I am a part of Lincoln High School, and Lincoln High School is forever a part of me." I went on to say that we would forever be connected because of our shared high school experiences (little did I know how true that would be over the years). My two opponents stood to the side of the podium, listening to me and glancing at the audience from time to time to see how they were perceiving my words.

"The importance of comradery, by supporting one another in all that we do, instead of competing against each other . . . You have my word that, as your student body president, I will do my best to highlight what unites us and not what makes us different. Thank you." And I walked away from the microphone to the sound of applause, whistles, shouts of praise, and recognition from the student body assembled on wood bleachers throughout the gymnasium. I was so proud, and not just because of the crowd's reaction, but because I had delivered the speech exactly how I wanted to after practicing countless times. I was prepared, and the suit my mom had made for me helped me feel even more confident.

I stood by to listen to my opponents' speeches as well, and I applauded them when they were done—although, to tell you the truth, it didn't sound like they had put as much effort into writing them as I had. I mean, they basically said a few words and that was it. I figured it was because they didn't take this position as seriously as I did, so why bother, right? I knew how much hard work had gone into writing and perfecting my speech, the many late nights I had spent rehearsing, making sure my tone was friendly but professional, approachable while relatable, and that my words were correct so as not to be misinterpreted. I knew how much time I had spent in actually talking to my fellow students, sitting down with them in the cafeteria or after school to ask them what they wanted from our school and in what ways they needed me to help them. I cherished these moments because they opened my eyes to the beauty of change that can happen when we reach out to our own community—and I believe this feeling is one of the reasons why I eventually established my career in public service. I was sure that my audience could sense how I much I wanted to be elected as their president. I mean, of course they could tell the difference between my speech and the others'. And of course they would want somebody who showed them just how much she cared for this role, not just the title.

I have to be honest though; I was apprehensive. One of the opponents was part of the Associated Student Body (ASB) clique. They were a tight-knit group—I knew I was a popular student, and I found it easy and natural to connect with people, but I did not take the ASB affiliation for granted. Would they really want to welcome a female African American student body president in their group? I doubted it. And that's why I expressed my concern to the principal, who was an African American man. Funny thing is, not only did he concur, but he told me that he had already planned to keep a close watch on the vote count to make sure it was going to be a fair process. And I believed him.

After the first vote count, one of the opponents was eliminated so there had to be runoff. When the results of the election came in, I didn't win. As disappointed as

I was in the outcome, I knew that this was the decision my fellow students had made, and I had to respect it. So, I delivered a short concession speech.

"I wish to congratulate our new student body president," I said. "I know that we are going to work together this year to make sure that every student in this school feels heard, validated, and supported. I know this will be a great year for us all!"

After my speech, my English teacher, a petite woman with short-cropped, ash blond hair, who appeared to be in her sixties, sought me out to share some words of wisdom and encouragement.

"I am sorry you didn't win," she said. "I have admired your drive and the lengths you went through to truly let students feel your presence and commitment. Sometimes, for girls and women, even when you are the best, even when you deserve to win, it just doesn't happen. It's a difficult life lesson, but don't give up on your goals because of a setback." She was just as disappointed by my loss as I was and clearly felt compelled to see me continue on in my endeavors and not give up. Several months later, I was very honored and gratified when I was chosen by my peers to keynote our senior baccalaureate because the students found me to be motivating and inspirational.

And, although I didn't see it as a life lesson at the time, I can assure you that this very moment of losing the election for student body president flashed right before my eyes when the mayor told me I wasn't one of the top three candidates for chief of police. And that's when my teacher's words clicked. It was indeed a life lesson, one that proved to me that no matter how hard you work, no matter how hard you commit to a position, you will not always come out on top even when you seemingly deserve to. But it is also what you do after your loss that is just as important as what you did when you campaigned for yourself, your values, and goals. And do you know why it's so important? Because the people who believed in you and were there to support you before you lost will still believe in you and will still be there to lift you up after your loss, reminding you that this moment does not define who you are.

## Committing to Self-Discipline

Thankfully, I had plenty of people ready to cheer me up and cheer me on. Many of them I had met years prior when I joined the basketball and track teams. It would have been so easy for all the girls on the teams to compete against one another, to see which one of us stood out by winning more, being the most popular, scoring the most points, being the cutest, and so forth. But we did not. We cheered one another on, encouraged one another to do better, and supported one another when we didn't achieve the goal we had hoped for. We helped one another understand what we needed to work harder on and become better at. As a result, we built a strong, resilient, and competitive team where each person mattered equally.

The team was an entity we believed in and cared for. We knew we had a common goal to achieve, so there was no point in competing against one another because that would have only slowed us down and more than likely prevented us from achieving our team goal. We dedicated our free time to building our team's physical and mental strength by exercising before first period and in the afternoon—it was common to see the girls on the track team out on the track early in the morning, rain or shine, doing yoga, push-ups, leg lifts, and whatnot before the other kids even got to school. All our hard work paid off when we set the record for the 400-meter relay, a record that lasted for twenty-eight years.

## Standing Up for What Is Right

I believe one of the secrets to our success was that we were friends and supporters both on and off the track. We loved spending time together after school and on weekends, and trust me when I tell you that there were life lessons to learn off the track too. I remember one time, Tracy, a White girl who was an ace at distance running, invited me and Vonda, another Black girl, to a party our classmates were having.

"The party is in the woods," Tracy explained. "And since I don't know how to get there, we'll just follow one of them with my car."

Vonda and I agreed and got into Tracy's car. It was springtime and just the right temperature outside where you needed to wear an extra layer early in the morning or late in the afternoon. But during the day, the Pacific Northwest breeze was warm enough that it allowed you to take that coat off and enjoy the weather—as if begging you for forgiveness after a harsh, long, and cold winter . . . and you know what? It worked every darn time! Anyway, I rolled down the window of the back seat to enjoy the breeze, knowing that by the time we arrived at the house in the woods it was probably going to be the time of day when we had to put on that extra layer. The car in front of us was guiding us at a steady pace, and Tracy followed it religiously through the woods, an area I had never been to before and was trying hard not to get spooked by—let's face it, most horror stories are set in an outlandish and seemingly desolated woodland, so you can't fault me for feeling uneasy. All of a sudden, the car in front of us slowed down and parked to the side of the road. Tracy followed suit.

"What's going on?" Vonda asked, slightly extending her neck forward to get a better view from her passenger's side.

"I have no clue," Tracy said.

Then the two guys in the car in front of us got out and signaled Tracy to go meet them by their car.

"All right," Tracy said, opening the door and walking toward them.

Vonda and I stayed back in the car, silent, watching. The three of them were talking and, judging by Tracy's body language—she kept glancing back at us, her arms crossed, shaking her head no—it wasn't a pleasant conversation.

*Something's wrong*, I thought.

Then one of the guys pointed at the car we were in and yelled, "Not two!"

"Not two, what?" Vonda wondered out loud.

Suddenly, I had this sinking feeling that we were not going to go to the party anymore.

Then Tracy stormed back toward us. And let me tell you, she was walking *with purpose*! She looked like she was stomping the whole way back, shaking her head the entire time. The guys had gotten back into their car and had turned the engine on. They seemed ready to leave without us.

"*Un*believable!" Tracy yelled as she got back into the driver's seat, her frustration conveyed by how hard she marked the prefix.

"What's happening?" I asked.

"Ugh . . . they said that they don't want two Black girls at this party."

Oh.

"*What?*" Vonda said in a high-pitched tone.

Tracy shook her head and looked down, as if in disbelief.

"Well, all right," I said. "Let's go home then."

At that, both Tracy and Vonda turned back to look at me, their raised eyebrows and slightly parted lips telling me that my response surprised them. And not in a good way.

"What?" I asked, not understanding their death stare. "If they don't want Vonda and me to go, then take us back home." I did not want to borrow trouble, and I did not want to be where I was not wanted. "What's wrong with that?"

"Everything is wrong with that!" Vonda said.

"Yeah, I know, but what can we do about it?" I asked, even more confused.

"I'll tell you what we *can* and *will* do about it," Tracy said, marking her words with her index finger—something that reminded me of when my mother scolded me for doing something the wrong way. "We are going to this damn party, whether they like it or not!"

"*What?*" Now I was the high-pitched one.

"Carmen," Vonda said. "Nobody is going to tell us that we can't go to a party because of the color of our skin, you hear me?"

I nodded.

Tracy turned the car on and began driving in the direction of the other car. Soon after, we arrived at a clearing in the woods with a bonfire and *a lot* of beer and joined the party. Nobody mentioned anything about Vonda and me being there, but there were a few subtle looks I caught that made me feel as though my presence wasn't that welcomed. Still, Tracy, Vonda, and I had a great time hanging out with one another and chatting with others. We left before the party was over—we had strict a curfew and we knew better than to miss it! The entire time I was there, I was very conscious that some people did not want me there, and of course, that niggling thought continued until we figured we had proved our point and it was time to go.

During the drive home, though, I could think only that my first reaction to what those guys said had been to oblige their request. I didn't question it. I didn't fight it. Even though I knew it was wrong of them to prevent us from attending a party because of our skin color. Vonda was outraged. Tracy was outraged. They stood up for themselves. They stood up for me. And I was so thankful to them. Their reaction made me understand that running away from racism is not going to put an end to it. No, the way to fight it is to face it. Quite a few times in my career on the police force, I found myself in situations I perceived as threatening to my morals, my beliefs, or even worse, my life. And I'll be honest, when I had to decide between fight or flight, so to speak, I often thought back on this story. That day, in that car, I learned that unless you're willing to stand up for what you believe is right, things are never going to change.

Indeed, the example set by my mother and the girls I had the privilege of becoming friends with during high school—and with whom I am still friends to this day—shaped my inner being and helped me become the woman, mother, and community server I am today. The lessons I learned at home, at school, on the track and basketball teams, as well as in my everyday life, taught me to work hard in order to succeed, to face failure with dignity, and to fight for what I believe to be right and fair.

# TACTICAL DEBRIEF

**WHAT DO LEADERSHIP,** racism, and sexism have in common? They don't start in the workplace. And they don't end in the workplace either. Leadership is not a skill you build when you receive that coveted promotion. Racism is not a reality you face only once you start climbing the corporate ladder. Sexism is not a malady faced only by women who work in male-dominated career fields. No.

Leadership is a skill whose seed is planted inside of you during childhood by watching people around you work hard and strive to better themselves. Just as my mother did. Racism is a reality whose seed is planted inside of you during childhood by people who believe that skin color is the only way to differentiate between the predominant binaries in our society: good and bad, right and wrong, superior and inferior. Where do you think those guys learned to say sentences like "We don't want two Black girls at the party"? Certainly not from Vonda or Tracy! Sexism is a malady whose seed is planted inside of you during childhood by people who believe that you can't do it just because you're a woman. Go and tell that to my friends on the track team, whose record held for close to three decades!

See what I mean? It all starts in the household. We learn the most important leadership lessons during childhood. The only way to change what doesn't work in our society is to change the way we behave behind closed doors. Being a leader is not a part-time effort that begins and ends at work. It's a way of life that must be taken care of, protected, and cherished even when we think nobody is watching. 'Cause let me tell you a secret: there's always somebody watching, even if it's a five-year-old boy who's walking to school with his bigger sister and is no longer shivering from the bitter cold of a Pacific Northwest winter thanks to an extra pair of handsewn gloves.

So now I want you to think of your own household. Go back to your childhood and think of what you learned by watching people of authority—parents, schoolteachers, sports coaches, and so forth. Think of the lessons you learned by hanging out with your peers on a Friday night, while driving to a party, or competing on the track team.

1. What are the most important leadership lessons you have learned through them?
2. How did they shape you into becoming the person you are today?
3. Are you leading by example in your own household?
4. What values and beliefs are you planting inside the people who look up to you?

# 2

# Genuine Relationships Are Important

Relationships are everything. Simple as that. The relationships I built and the friendships I developed during my high school years were crucial to my development as a person because they showed me that hard work is vital to keep moving forward and making progress. My teammates and I trained tirelessly and bonded over our shared love of sports, dedication to school spirit, commitment to our team, and to one another. But we also had many things in common off the track, as we were all from the same town, attended church, and gathered at the local ice cream shop. The bond we shared was so strong that it stood the test of time, and we are dear friends still to this day—our latest get-together immortalized in photos that we proudly showed our family members, posted on our social media accounts, and used as an entryway to share stories of the good ole days and relive experiences of youth that make the heart tingle with joyful memories.

But while the peers I surrounded myself with as a teenager shaped and influenced my values and beliefs, it was the relationships I developed while serving in the US Army with people from different walks of life and different cultural backgrounds that taught me important lessons that would prove to be invaluable as I advanced in my career. By confronting different realities, personalities, and social etiquettes, I learned the value of adaptability, the true power of teamwork, and the importance of respecting boundaries and appreciating diversity.

## The Value of Adaptability

"Mom, don't get mad, but . . ." I told my mother over the phone. I could tell by her silence she was ready to get mad. Really mad. After all, what else could I expect her reaction to be if I started my sentence the way I did, am I right? I took a deep breath and just spilled it out: "I'm going to stay in the army."

"You *what?*"

*Theeeere it is,* I thought as I braced myself for impact.

"Girl, have you lost your precious mind?" my mom said as I heard my father in the background ask her, "What's going on?"

"Mom, hear me out . . ." I hoped she'd be receptive to my choice.

"You got so many track and field scholarship offers to Annapolis, Bellevue Community College, Eastern Washington University," she went on and on, speaking so fast she reminded me of those people at the end of pharmaceutical commercials listing all the side effects. "This army stint was supposed to be a summer thing, not a career choice!"

She was right. The Advanced Individual Training was indeed supposed to be a summer program as part of my ROTC program at college, but once there I enjoyed the challenges and comradery and wanted to continue.

"Don't you remember the sacrifices your father—and *all* of us—made when he was in the army? Is this the life you really want for yourself? You better get back to college right now or else I'm going to—"

"Mom, listen!" I interrupted her, regretting it immediately—she had raised me better than that.

"Mm-hmm," she muttered. I took it as both a good and a bad sign, as if she was telling me: "I'm going to let you talk for now, but you're going to get another earful soon enough, lady!"

And on I went, making my case.

Surprisingly enough, she didn't make a big fuss and just let me go deal with the consequences of my own decisions.

And boy, did I face consequences right away!

"Carmen, where do you think you're going with this trunk full of stuff?" my recruiter admonished me when he saw the fully packed trunk I had taken with me.

I looked at him, then at my trunk, then back at him. "What?" I shrugged. "I need all of my stuff," I said nonchalantly.

He gave *one* look. And I wish there were enough words to describe that *one* look. Lips tightly sealed together, arms crossed, and eyes that didn't blink. Get the picture? So, I did the only thing I could think of.

"Mom, I need your help," I said, feeling like I was six years old all over again and had insisted on doing a task all by myself to prove to my mother that I was a big girl and then ended up being unable to complete it, eyes filled with tears of bruised pride, and going to seek help from her. The one person I insisted had to let me just do things my way.

That night, my mother came to the hotel where we were staying because we had an early morning flight to our military base. Together, we went through everything I brought (all sorts of needless cosmetics and clothes) and packed the essentials in a much smaller bag. The next day, after she left to go back home with all the things (literally a trunk full) that the army considered to be extras and, therefore, unnecessary, I got on a flight heading to Fort McClellan, Alabama.

Once there, dozens of women processed in, receiving shots, equipment, uniforms, paperwork, and so on. We then boarded buses that took us to what would be our new home for the next few months: the white-washed, trimmed-in-dark-green, very unimpressive barracks. The bus stopped and this mean-looking guy got on and started yelling: "You've got *five* seconds to get off the bus!"

I looked around at the other women and wondered who this guy was, why he was yelling, and if he had lost his mind. Oh, I forgot to mention: it was summertime. Alabama in the summer. And I was brought up just near Seattle, Washington. I'm going to leave it at that.

*Get off the bus in five seconds!?* I thought. It felt like it was a million degrees outside!

"You've got five seconds to get off the bus and four have already gone!" he yelled again, as the women hustled, frantically grabbing their gear and fleeing the bus, and I was starting to feel kinda lonely and in the spotlight because I felt like he was talking to me now.

"*Get off! Get off! Get off!*" he yelled. And the only other woman on that bus jumped out of her skin and off her seat and quickly got off the bus.

*You have got to be kidding me!* I was this itty-bitty person, and I had been sweating while sitting down. Imagine if I actually got out in that Alabama heat and humidity. I would have melted in no time. But this guy just wouldn't shut up. So I got up, grabbed my bag, and meandered toward him.

As I passed by him, he made sure to point out I was the last person to follow orders.

I got off the bus thinking, *Whatever, you're crazy!*

And I kept walking, rather slowly, until I heard, "Private! Where do you think you're going?"

"I'm headed to the—" I pointed to where he told the other women to go, but he interrupted me before I could finish my sentence.

"You better pick it up and start moving!" he yelled at the top of his lungs.

"Okay, I'm going, I'm going," I said, my tone revealing all my naivete of military life.

"Go! Go! Go!"

He yelled again, convincing me it was time to pick up my pace.

"Faster! Faster!"

"Okay! I'm going." At this point I was in a full run toward the other women, who had figured out before me that we were supposed to sprint to the barracks. Yikes! Carrying all our gear and sprinting in the Alabama midday heat! What was I in for?

Once in formation, the drill sergeant told us what was expected of us. Then, he told us to run.

And this time, I didn't put up a fight.

But let me tell you, military training is serious business. The next morning, we were woken up at 3:30 a.m. to do our daily physical training. And because it was Alabama and it was summertime, we couldn't exercise in the grass because of the ticks, chiggers, and all the other bugs that thrive in that kind of environment. So we had to exercise on gravel. And *that* was not fun.

No sir, no ma'am.

But I did it anyway, of course, and I was proud of myself for powering through that. Until I made the mistake of venting about it with my mother. And not a little. No, I dramatized.

"Mom, you should see what they have us do here," I said in an unnecessarily agitated tone. "They have us do push-ups on *rocks*! And these rocks are digging into your hands. This is hard, Mom."

And did I stop there? Nope. I continued and added more colorful details, heightening the drama. I probably made it sound as if I were being forced to climb Mount Everest in the worst weather with no gear.

So what did my mom do?

Well, she called the base commander and complained about the training we were being forced to do.

"They have those young girls out there doing hard, *hard* exercise. My daughter is telling me that her hands are all cut up on those rocks."

And what did the base commander do?

Take a guess.

"Private Fulghum!" the sergeant called me one day. "I understand that your mom called the base commander. Every time you see me, just drop and me give me ten." Meaning I was to drop to the ground and do ten push-ups.

It didn't take me long to figure out that my mom's chat with the base commander was having an effect, but not what she had in mind. One thing I knew for sure was that I would not be telling my mother any more negative stories about my experience—what a backfire!

*Great job, Carmen!* I thought to myself.

From that day onward, every time he walked in a room or I saw him somewhere else on base, I dropped and did push-ups, without him even telling me anything: "One, drill sergeant," and, "Two, drill sergeant," all the way until ten. And although it was supposed to be a punishment, it soon became rather funny, especially when surrounded by people who had no idea what was happening and why it was happening. To put in a bit more flavor and humor, I added a beat and a bit of crescendo and decrescendo by almost shouting out the number as if marked by a hand clap and then deepening my tone.

"*One*—drill—sergeant."

"*Two*—drill—sergeant."

"*Three*—drill—sergeant."

And so forth.

"Stop singing to me. Stop singing!" the drill sergeant said every time I did the singsong.

By the time I could stop doing push-ups as soon as I saw him, the whole base was in on it, and they all had a good laugh every time they heard my push-up sing-along.

But I remember the months I spent training in the military fondly because they taught an invaluable lesson: To advance in life—whether in your career or just as a human being—you have to adapt by following directions and going through what you have to go through, even if it's uncomfortable. Even if it's painful. Cutting corners won't do you any good. And I learned that lesson the hard way.

## The True Power of Teamwork

In life, it's so easy to forget that it's not all about us. Did the mailman deliver your mail to your neighbor's mailbox? Instead of rolling your eyes and scoffing over it because it inconvenienced you, pause for a moment and think: What if he received some devastating personal news that obfuscated his mind so much that he absentmindedly placed your letters in the wrong mailbox? Did your colleague make a mistake you know will jeopardize her chances at a promotion you are also hoping to get? Instead of highlighting her mistake to gain advantage over her in the race up the corporate ladder, how about you talk to her privately and help her solve it?

Yes, we are all individuals, and we are all different. But we are also human beings sharing a short portion of time together on this planet. So why focus our energy exclusively on ourselves when we could help other members of society who are just trying to do what they can and cope the best way they can with whatever physical, emotional, or mental obstacle they face? If the pandemic has taught us anything it is that, as the whole world whispered in unison, we are all in this together.

I have always been a firm believer in teamwork. In the previous chapter, you learned where I built team spirit. And it was my experience on the track team in high school that helped me become the squad leader while at basic training in Alabama.

I remember one time, during one of our long bivouacs, I noticed a girl in my group struggling with her rucksack. It seemed to be too heavy for her, especially judging how hunched her back was, how much she was struggling for breath, and how slowly she was walking, unable to keep up with the rest of us. Physically, she was smaller than us—thin and a bit shorter. So I had a choice to make: let her struggle through—and probably have her fail the training—or help her out?

It was a no-brainer for me.

"Listen," I said to the other six members of my squad. "Here's what we're going to do: she is struggling with carrying that rucksack and we are going to help her with it. We are going to each carry her backpack for ten minutes. We need to give her a break and get it off her back. And we will help her with it because we are a team."

I was expecting at least one person to cross her arms and refuse to do extra work. Because, after all, why should they do extra work? It's not their fault that a team member wasn't able to keep up with the rest of us, right? But to my surprise, not one of them complained or griped.

So as we marched uphill, we took turns and carried her backpack along with our own rucksack. Once we reached our destination, I felt such pride. Not because my squad followed my lead, but because they each engaged in the mission, and we reached our destination successfully. One of our own needed our help and support in completing the mission, and we all showed up for it. As a team.

## The Importance of Respecting Boundaries and Appreciating Diversity

Growing up, I was always surrounded by the same people: my family members and high school friends. We knew one another well enough to get the inside jokes, understand when one of us was having a bad day without even having to ask, and respect our likes and dislikes. This is what happens when you are raised in the same place your whole childhood and teenage years. You build a routine, habits, and memories.

But when I went to Alabama, I found myself being part of a group of people from all walks of life and different cultural backgrounds. Suddenly, I was no longer around people who had many things in common with me. The women I shared a room with, for example, came from different parts of the country and had different priorities and sets of values. If one found a joke to be funny, the other found it offensive. If one found the food to be disgusting, the other found it delicious, just like her mother made it. If one found it important to pray every night before going to bed, the other found it ridiculous to pray to an invisible entity that allowed wars and cancer to happen.

In a nutshell: I came face-to-face with diversity. And when you are surrounded by so much diversity—of race, thought, religion, and education—it is essential to understand and respect one another's boundaries, or you could find yourself at the center of an awkward and uncomfortable situation. Like that one time when a girl referred to someone's race and another girl began fuming with rage.

"Listen," I whispered to her. "I get it, but there is no reason to let your rage lead you to a confrontation—that will end up negatively. Let her know why you are offended and why you found it disrespectful to you and your culture."

I tried calming her down. More than likely, she had been on the receiving end of many derogatory or discriminatory racial remarks and was sensitive to them. She had clearly had enough and was no longer going to stand for it. And as important as it was that the girl who made the comment understood that it came across as offensive to at least one person in the room, it was also crucial that the one who was hurt by it understood that not everybody was out to get her. Eventually, things calmed down and the two of them spoke about it in private.

Being in basic training with people raised differently eased us new recruits into the reality of the world, and soon I was sent to Seoul, South Korea, which was the biggest and most densely populated city I had ever been in, with a population hovering around ten million. From there I was stationed in Daegu, with around two million people. And *that* was really a cultural shock! I thought that having to face diversity on base was challenging—without realizing that, as different as we all were, at least we were all from the United States of America, spoke the same language, and followed the same social etiquette. But when I arrived in the Asian country, I was faced with diversity with a capital *D*. Once there, the first thing I had to do was attend a class on Korean culture, an orientation to make sure I learned the ABCs of the country's dos and don'ts.

I wish that had been enough. But, as most often in life, I learned my lessons by trial and error. And it wasn't always pretty. I got my initiation into the Korean culture when, after having just landed in the country, I was crossing an incredibly busy street—I think it was eight lanes wide. People kept bumping into me, and I kept on saying—in English, of course—"Excuse me, I'm sorry," in a failed effort to make my presence known so that people would allow me to walk by unharmed. Did they even turn to look at me and apologize? Nope. But that was absolutely normal behavior for people living in a bustling, densely populated city. No one was apologizing for incidental bumping into or contact with others while crossing the street. Over the course of my one-year stay in Korea, I learned that blowing my nose in public was a big no-no, but sniffing in public was socially accepted. A biggie was taking off your shoes before entering a home. My age also didn't match the one on my documents because, in Korea, time in the womb is the first year of life—which meant that, in Korea, I was about a year older than I was in the United States. But age wasn't the only difference between the culture I grew up in and the one that I now faced daily.

"Have you noticed that women don't drive cars?" a fellow soldier pointed out to me one day while walking downtown.

"Really?" I said, looking around to see if I could spot a female driver. "You're right." I saw plenty of women in cars but always as passengers, never as drivers. It was 1985 and I couldn't understand why women didn't drive in South Korea. Were they just not allowed? Was it a preference? Social etiquette? Who knew?

Indeed, trying to keep up with all the unfamiliar norms proved to be challenging. But as a guest in their country, I needed to adapt to their customs to show them the respect they deserved. Before long, you wouldn't catch me blowing my nose in public or expecting the person who bumped into me to turn around and apologize. And regardless of all the small or big differences between American and Korean culture, I also learned that there are many similarities: both peoples enjoy sharing a good meal together, having a genuine laugh, and working hard to provide for their family. It was astonishing to me to see that I was so far away from my own home yet so close to the values I believed in.

When it came time for me to leave South Korea, I remember taking one last look at Daegu from the plane during liftoff and smiling. This densely populated city, with its many quirks and perks, had taught me that there were different ways to see the world and different ways to live your life. And I was glad I adapted to the differences, because my own cultural awareness was now richer and more developed than when I had first landed in that faraway land.

After Korea, I was sent to Germany for a few weeks. I remember when I told my mother about my new assignment, she made a comment that I was clearly following in my father's footsteps because he, too, had been to Germany a few times. I was thrilled about my assignment because it felt as though I had come full circle: I spent a few years in Germany as a little girl and now I was going to spend three weeks as a grown woman and a soldier of the US Army! How cool was that?

Anyway, just like in Korea, in Germany we attended the introductory class on German culture. But Korea had taught me that there was only one way to truly learn about a culture: hang out with its people! So off I went mingling with the locals. One evening, I was invited to a dinner with a few German friends I had made. Laid out on a long wooden table—self-service style, so to speak— were big pans filled with some type of boiled meat. The smell was quite familiar to me as it reminded me of home, in particular of Sundays spent at church. But I could not pinpoint the aroma from afar. So I walked closer to see what it was, and lo and behold there it was: ham hock!

"Are you okay, Carmen?" a young German soldier whom I'd recently befriended and who spoke English very well asked me. "You don't like to eat pork?"

"Oh." I realized that my speechlessness at the sight of ham hock prompted him to believe that I was not grateful for what was being offered for dinner. So I quickly set the record straight: "I love ham hocks! I am surprised, because back home, in the States, this is considered the food of the poor as it is not the best part of the animal, you know?"

"Really?" His raised eyebrows conveyed his surprise. "We use this part of the pig often in German cuisine. It is actually popular in European cuisine in general, not just German. I remember eating it one time in Italy with baked potatoes and peas—delicious!"

I looked at him and thought that back home I was used to seeing ham hocks mainly in African American cuisine, as soul food. Eating ham hock is a tradition that dates back to slavery: when slave owners ate pork, they would leave all the fattier parts of the animal to the slaves—shoulder, ham hock, feet, neck, and so forth—as those cuts were considered less desirable. As a result, those scraps became part of our identity and tradition, a meal filled with so much heart that it just enriched your soul every time you ate it.

"Shall we eat?" he asked, offering me a plate.

"Can't wait!" I began filling my plate and smiling at the thought of eating soul food in Germany.

After three weeks, I was back on an airplane heading back to the United States of America. Once again, I smiled as I thought back on my time overseas, the people I met, and the differences that separated American and German culture as well as the many similarities that united them.

# TACTICAL DEBRIEF

**MEETING NEW PEOPLE** and building relationships with them is the best way to confront the realities of the world. Cultural differences challenge you to become more aware of the world and what other people go through. They push you to see the other not as a menace to your safety and stability but as a way to enrich your own cultural awareness and evolve as an individual. Adapting to other cultures and lifestyles will prove to be both difficult and exciting, because it is through those tests that you will learn so much more about your personality and the role you play in the world.

Exposing yourself to other ways to live will build resiliency and will open your mind to new possibilities, as you expand your horizons and welcome new people, language, and yes, even ways to cook unfamiliar food. It is through those relationships that you not only grow as a person but also learn to appreciate others. Essentially, meeting people different from me in basic training and throughout my military career—especially people I met abroad—taught me an invaluable lesson, one that I would eventually apply to my own leadership style: respect for other people's values and boundaries.

As a leader, it is pivotal that you learn how to respect others in their diversity, whether it be cultural, religious, or sexual. We are all different, but it is our differences that make us who we are. And it is who we are that helps us build a successful team. And it is a successful team that will power through and complete the mission, no matter how challenging it is.

And now, it's your turn to think of the value of adaptability, the true power of teamwork, and the importance of respecting boundaries and appreciating diversity.

1.  When was the first time you found yourself having to adapt to a set of rules you did not understand at first but then learned to follow and appreciate?
2.  Can you think of a time when teamwork proved to be invaluable to completing an important task?
3.  How do you set boundaries in your personal and professional life?
4.  Do you find it challenging to understand diversity and respect other people's boundaries? Or do you welcome cultural, religious, and sexual differences within both your personal and professional life?

# 3

# Keep Your Mentors, Allies, and Sponsors Close

No one knows everything—although plenty of people think they do. Truth is, we all need help. And it's not because of our cultural background, gender, or ethnicity. No, it's much simpler than that. It's because nobody who has ever achieved any level of success, whether in their private or professional life, has been able to do it alone. If you look closer, you will find that behind all accomplished people—whether CEO or employee, store manager or store clerk, and so forth—there are mentors, allies, and sponsors who have played a crucial role in their lives.

Who are these mentors, allies, and sponsors, you ask? They are the people who believe in you, who cheer you on, who praise you even when you are not in the room, who show you the way, who make sure you don't make their same mistakes, who open the door of opportunities to you, and who pull a chair around so you can have a seat at the table. In a nutshell: they are the relationships we build throughout our lives.

Mentors, allies, and sponsors are not interchangeable titles, as they do not play the same role. Mentors are people in your same career field who coach you and guide you, especially when you are first starting out. Mind you, though, that it is not the responsibility of the lower-ranking person to find a mentor. Rather, it is the responsibility of more seasoned people to find a newcomer who would benefit from their experiences. A mentor is the senior editor who coaches the junior editor, the master sergeant who coaches the airman, the teacher who coaches the teacher's teacher.

Allies are people who know you, know your work, and sing your praises to others. They aren't always the ones helping you directly get that next job, but they are the ones making sure people know about the good work you are doing, as they help ensure you get credit where credit is due. As you build relationships through hard work and engagement, you will naturally develop allies.

And, last but not least, there are sponsors. They are the folks who open doors so you can follow them through and have a chance to lead the organization. They are the people who invest their personal capital in you, those who know just how important it is to ensure that all their hard work does not stop with them when they move up in the organization or retire but instead continues to flourish and improve through the person they choose to sponsor.

In my life, I have been lucky enough to have had many mentors, allies, and sponsors. I honestly don't think I would have achieved everything I have achieved had it not been for their support and guidance. And let me tell you, some of the most important lessons I learned from my mentors, allies, and sponsors did not come with a big pink bow on top and shiny sparkles. Nope, they came in the form of a bitter remark, a confrontation, or the proverbial smack on the hand. And it didn't feel good. Now, I could have easily dismissed them and said that I knew better and that they were just a bunch of people full of themselves, old-timers with no life who just didn't want us younger people to succeed because we refused to play by their rules.

But I didn't. I didn't let my ego win. Because even my own mother taught me some of the most important lessons in my life using a higher tone of voice, a strict curfew, and firm boundaries. But it was thanks to her higher tone of voice that I stopped being stubborn and started listening to what she had to say, and these conversations usually included the universal signature phrase of a loving parent: "It's for your own good." It was through that strict curfew that I did not find myself in dangerous situations and got enough rest so I could perform better in school and sports. It was through those firm boundaries that I got my priorities straight by putting education first, committing to my team, and still finding time to tend to my hobbies.

So pay attention to the lesson you are being taught, without letting your ego get in the way. Welcome the guidance of people who have been there before you, without thinking that you know better—you don't. And honor your mentors, allies, and sponsors by becoming one for people who come after you.

## Meet My Mentors

I was fresh out of the academy, and I had just started working at the police department in Seattle. As any other police officer will tell you, I clearly remember my very first call as if it were yesterday—there's just something about that first call you get as a new police officer; and when you think about it, you can still feel the adrenaline rushing through your veins. My first call was a run-of-the-mill disturbance call, which as a cop you quickly learn is never a run-of-the-mill disturbance call. No sir, no ma'am. I was itching to do good work, so I quickly got on the radio and said, "3G2, I'll take it."

I was new, I had no idea where this call was in the city, but I was amped up and making my way there. As I was driving there, the radio went off, saying, "We now have people fighting on scene."

*What the—*

"Shots fired!"

*Holy—*

"Person down!"

"Oh my . . ." I said, as my back suddenly felt both sweaty and cold. I had just jumped on a disturbance call, wanting to prove my worth, picturing myself going to peacefully talk to the neighbor who had his music a bit too loud for the eighty-year-old woman's ears, ending with the neighbors shaking hands and living happily ever after. Okay, that might have been an exaggeration. I didn't know what to expect, but it certainly wasn't *this*!

"3G2, set the staging area," my supervisor said over the radio.

"Copy."

Staging area? *I don't know where to go, and what is a staging area?!*

My adrenaline was pumping so hard I had forgotten all about what a staging area was and where to set it. I thought about grabbing the radio and asking my colleagues for guidance, but I was too proud to do that. I had jumped on this call, and now I didn't know how to get there. What to do: Expose my naivete and come clean or pretend I knew what I was doing and that I was not panicking at all and potentially risk the safety of those on the scene?

There was such chaos in my head that I barely noticed the terrifying silence on the air.

*Wait, where did everyone go?* I thought, hoping they hadn't disappeared and left me there alone.

"3G1, let's make the staging area one block west at 3200 block. Approach from north." One of my colleagues— and a more experienced police officer—instructed another cop to help me with setting the staging area so that, once I arrived on scene, I could take the report.

Once we handled the disturbance call and were back at the precinct, I thought I was going to *hear* about it—

like when I was a little girl and did or said something wrong in public and my mom gave me that look that screamed, "I'm being quiet now, but you're going to hear about it when we get home." But, to my surprise, nobody said anything negative. On the contrary, they complimented me for doing a good job and told me they knew I was a hard worker. They were very supportive and reassured me that this case had gone sideways quickly, and experience was going to be the only way to learn how to act. Fortunately for me, I had them as my mentors whose example I knew I would follow.

But as I mentioned before, not every lesson is delivered in sugar and spice and everything nice. Some of the most important lessons come coated in vinegar. Just like the lesson I learned from Pat Hayes.

"You keep coming in to work late, Officer Best," Sergeant Hayes admonished me one morning as I got to the police station. I checked my watch: five minutes late.

Dang, she was right. I was supposed to be there at three in the morning—that's when roll call was. Instead, I was five minutes late.

"I'm sorry, Sergeant." I pleaded my case. "I have a brand-new baby at home, and I ran late this morning."

"This is not the first you've been late though." She looked straight at me. I felt like I had nowhere to hide.

"I know and I'm sorry, but . . ." I sighed. "I woke up, took care of the baby, got her ready to go, dropped her off at my sister-in-law's house, then came to work," I said in a rather robotic tone as if I were reciting my grocery list by heart. My eyes were heavy with lost sleep and no rest. While a good listener, I was in no mood for a lecture. I was a brand-new police officer and a brand-new mom. To say that I felt like I had a million things to juggle at once would be a major understatement. I had so much to learn both in my career field and motherhood, and I had no idea just how much.

"Mm-hmm . . ." she said, taking a step closer to me. "Okay, so you are coming in a few minutes late."

*Phew, she gets it.*

Then, she glanced at my eyes and lips, squinted, and added: "But you found the time to put your mascara and lipstick on, huh?"

Busted.

And just when I thought she was going to add more, she gave me *one* look. Raised eyebrow, tilted head, pursed lips. "Blink, and you'll miss it" type of look. Then, she turned and walked away.

I was left speechless—and I'm never left speechless.

I walked to a desk, sat down, and thought of the conversation I just had with Sergeant Hayes. There I was, explaining how long it took me to get my baby ready, when in reality, I also prioritized my makeup routine.

To get all cutesy up for work was more of a priority to me than getting in this chair at 3:00 instead of 3:05.

And that was a hard pill to swallow. I looked around me and saw my colleagues hard at work. They got to work on time. Clearly, I needed to get my priorities straight. But as I looked around, I also noticed that I was mainly surrounded by White men in uniform. Sergeant Hayes had much more experience than I did and, as a result, knew just how hard it was for a woman to make it in a male-dominated career field. Simply put, women were the minority. So she wanted to make sure I knew what was at stake. It wasn't just about the five-minute tardiness. It was about the socially accepted narrative that women must choose between career and motherhood because society believes we can't have it all. It was about the fact that, in the 1980s, women made up less than 8 percent of the police force in the United States— in 2019, female officers made up 12.7 percent of law enforcement, not an impressive jump, if you ask me.[1] And it was also about the fact that, as a woman of color, I was even more of a minority within the minority.

I leaned back in my chair and nodded as I absorbed the lesson Sergeant Hayes had just taught me. She felt the responsibility to ensure that she was not going to be the last woman to become a police sergeant, which is why she became my mentor. Through her leadership, I learned that I, too, had to ensure that I was not going to be the last Black woman to become a police officer and chief, which is why I worked hard to reshape the Seattle police force by highlighting diversity in a way that mirrors the sociocultural and multiethnic landscape of our country.

And you bet I learned my lesson: get to work on time but keep wearing that mascara and lipstick!

## Meet My Allies

The day after Mayor Durkan told me I had not been selected as one of the top three candidates to be promoted to chief of police, I flew to Tennessee for a major city chiefs conference—a gathering of around sixty-nine major city police chiefs from all over the country, as well as vendors, academics, and people from the Department of Justice and other important law enforcement organizations. I remember when I got on the airplane on the tarmac of Seattle-Tacoma International Airport, I closed my eyes and took a deep, cleansing sigh.

The day before had been a whirlwind of emotions for me—exciting high highs and crushing low lows. Even though it was May, the weather was colder than usual in the Pacific Northwest, so the idea of going somewhere sunny and warm brought a smile to my face. Not to mention, I really needed this break. People in Seattle expected me to release even more statements, and to be honest, I didn't feel like it quite yet. I knew that something had gone terribly wrong in the selection process, and I planned on making another statement only once I learned more about what really happened behind the scenes.

"Good morning, ladies and gentlemen, this is your captain speaking." The deep voice on the intercom startled me. I opened my eyes and saw we were just about done boarding, which was my signal to turn my phone on airplane mode. The moment I took it out of my jacket side pocket, however, I saw the blinking blue line that alerted me of incoming emails.

*That's sweet*, I thought. Since the press conference the day before—which took place in the room next to the mayor's office—my phone had not stopped ringing for a minute. Emails, text messages, and phone calls from friends, family members, and colleagues who wanted to share their opinion of what probably happened during the selection process, to say how sorry they were that I did not make the top three, and to offer their support and appreciation for all that I had done for the community. So I was actually looking forward to reading these emails as I was expecting them to be from the same group of people who had first reached out to me. But when I checked the emails I had just received, I noticed they were mostly from reporters.

Ugh, now what? I suddenly felt a huge weight pushing my shoulders down. I clicked on one of them and—

"Cabin crew, prepare for takeoff."

Oops! It was time to go to Tennessee. I quickly turned my phone on airplane mode and made sure my seat belt was properly buckled and my seat was in the upright position. And before I knew it, Seattle became smaller and smaller as I admired the sleeping city from above. Until, in true northwestern fashion, the clouds took over and there was nothing left to see but the beauty of dawn shyly waking up the night sky.

The flight was uneventful—which is always a good thing. As soon as I landed, I turned the airplane mode off, and I was instantly flooded with emails, voice messages, and social media notifications.

"Is it true that you told the mayor you didn't want to be promoted to chief?" one email read.

"What?!" I said out loud, prompting the passenger sitting next to me to glance over. I gave her a polite smile to let her know I was fine. I wasn't fine, though. *Who would start such a ridiculous rumor?* I thought to myself. *Why would I, of all people, decline a promotion to chief when I have been serving as such for months now, not to mention how much I care about my community?*

I got off the plane so quickly, I didn't even notice the wall of heat and humidity that had welcomed me in Tennessee. As I walked toward the taxi area, I called the mayor herself to discuss the rumor.

"No, I never said that," she said.

I believed her because I later watched an interview in which a reporter asked her why I wasn't in the running, and the mayor replied, "You'll have to ask Carmen Best why." I could see how her answer fostered that assumption, whether or not that was the intent. And that's why I called her in the first place: to ensure that there was not a misconception that I was complicit in the decision to not be in the top three.

On the ride to the hotel, I must have read countless similar emails from more reporters, but I decided not to answer any of them. This could wait. Not to mention, I was truly looking forward to spending a day or two with fellow chiefs without having to talk about what was happening with the promotion back in Seattle.

But as luck would have it, the moment I stepped foot in the conference room, I felt as though I had been invited to attend a wake.

"Oh, Carmen, we are so sorry," said one.

"Oh, Carmen, this is terrible," said another.

"How could you *not* be in the final running for the position of chief?" questioned others.

Geez, I just wanted to come here, attend this conference, and not have to think about any of this. I guess it was too much to ask. But as tired as I was of hearing about it, I also felt my heart tingle with joy because I knew I had their support, and they were being genuine in expressing their disappointment. As much as I wanted to answer them in the most honest way I could, as much as I wanted to be in the doldrums, and as much as I wanted to shout from the rooftop that something *really* unfair must have taken place behind the scenes, that this felt like more than a microaggression because I would have been the first Black woman to cover the role—officially, since I had been the de facto chief for quite some time now—I knew I couldn't. And I didn't. I kept a stiff upper lip the entire time and focused on what I was there for, which was to talk about ways we could improve our departments and, as a result, our communities. So I tried cutting these conversations short by simply offering a slight smile and saying: "Well, decisions have been made, things happen. There's nothing we can do about it."

But what I did not know at the time was that many people actually were trying to do *something* about it. Who were these people? My allies.

Many people—both inside and outside the police department—expressed their disdain about me not being considered for the position of chief. I heard that Karinda Harris and Vivian Phillips, who had been leading the public uproar to support me, took charge and began lobbying friends and community members while I was in Tennessee, collecting signatures and urging them to call the mayor so as to have my name put back on the list. Former mayoral candidate Nikkita Oliver took to her Twitter account to address the situation by tagging Mayor Durkan and writing: "This racist mess will not stand. Are you that uncomfortable with Black people, let alone a Black woman, being in a position of influence?"[2] Lisa Daugaard, community police commission member, also took to her social media to invite Mayor Durkan to correct the irregularities that had taken place in the process of selecting the top three candidates.

Still utterly unaware of the uproar happening behind the scenes, on Monday I was back in Seattle and back to work. Although I was disappointed in the way that the selection had taken place, I knew that I had a big responsibility of helping the top three candidates become acquainted with the department, introducing them to people they needed to meet to guarantee the best and smoothest transition, and ensuring they all had an executive protection detail to drive them around the city.

Days went by and I was back to the regularly scheduled programming when, one morning in the paper, I came across a letter to the editor I was most certainly *not* expecting to read. I sat up straight in my chair, quickly placed the cup full of hot coffee on my desk—spilling some of my morning beverage on the oak—and stretched out the newspaper page. The letter was written by R. Gil Kerlikowske, whom I consider an ally and advocate. He'd been Seattle's chief of police from 2000 to 2009 and was in India at the time—something I knew because, even though we had not spoken in about two years, the police world is small, and people are able to easily keep up with what is happening to those of us who are lucky enough to gain tenure. So I knew he was on another continent and knew I hadn't been considered for the top three.

In his letter he expressed his disdain and disappointment regarding the decision and highlighted how my career as an army veteran, a community server, and a dedicated police officer were important qualifications. He also urged the mayor to review the decision and place my name back on the list of potential candidates. I had a hard time reading that letter, and not just because my hand was trembling as a I held the newspaper but because my vision was blurry due to the tears in my eyes. To have somebody I looked up to stand up for me in such an impassioned and public way when he had absolutely nothing to gain showed me that perhaps I had left just as much of a mark in his life as he did in mine. For him to take time out of his day, while in India, to write a letter to the editor and make his voice heard about an issue that did not even involve him or his reputation or his career meant the world to me. I reached for a tissue and carefully dried my tears as I took controlled breaths in and out.

And this was how I learned of the uproar that had been taking place in Seattle, a city very much divided on so many issues but that somehow came together to support me. The community I had served all these years made sure that the city knew where it stood. Director of the Vietnamese Community Leadership Institute Linh Thai publicly expressed her wish to see my name back on the list; Chinatown-International District public safety coordinator Sonny Nyugen and Pastor Lawrence Willis from the Truevine of Holiness Missionary Baptist Church also came forward to voice the community's concern with my dismissal.

People I had met and helped over the years shared their stories, like the woman whose son was murdered for being gay. When she spoke up about our encounter, I felt tears rushing to my eyes. Her son and another man were sitting in a parked car outside her house. A guy lured them to that very spot through text messages and murdered them both in cold blood. After the tragedy and after all information had been gathered by detectives and officers, I decided to go visit her. Not just as a member of law enforcement but as a mother, first and foremost. I found that her daughter and other family members were present, too, so I sat down with all of them, listened to them, and offered words of support. Although I had stayed in touch with her as I checked on her well-being from time to time, it truly humbled me to see just how much my small gesture of simply listening to her grief, as well as to her many wonderful stories about her son, meant to her.

As the community came together, I realized that I was not the only one feeling as though something unjust had happened behind closed doors, something that I would categorize under the long, long list of microaggressions that marginalized communities, underrepresented communities, and that minorities often face every single day. The general sense in the community seemed to be that racism—and perhaps even sexism—had played a major part in the decision-making process. And while Seattle's race demographic is indeed primarily White, the African American, Asian American, Native American, and Hispanic communities still make up a large part of the population. And it seemed to me that the community's collective reaction was a loud cry for equality, validation, and representation.

Six weeks after the press conference announcing the names of the top three candidates, one dropped out of the running and my name replaced his. On August 13, 2018, at city hall, after a whirlwind of public upheaval and recanted decisions, I was sworn in officially as chief of police of Seattle.

"You've managed to pull in a wide range of folks," said Councilmember Mike O'Brien at the ceremony.

I acknowledged his statement with a smile and, addressing the audience, said: "I had no idea I had so much support in the community." As the crowd applauded, I turned to my left to quickly look at my daughters, who were standing a few steps behind me, a twinkle of pride in their eyes and shy smiles on their faces. In that moment, I couldn't help hoping that my selection would help my daughters and their future children—as well as everyone else, for that matter—not have to face such an uphill battle in order to have their qualifications properly recognized and validated. I hoped that my selection would usher in a new era when people of any gender and color didn't have to rely on public turmoil to have their experience and competence equally valued and considered. I looked back at the crowd and saw a few of them smiling, a few of them still clapping, and a few of them with tight lips but a hopeful gaze. Each one of them different from the next, each one of them with their own set of goals and troubles, yet all there for the common purpose of using their voice to bring on change. It was not lost on me that the community had just placed a huge responsibility on my shoulders, but I knew I could not possibly do it alone. Yes, I would be counting on the support of fourteen hundred officers and six hundred support staff, but I also knew that I needed members of the community to help. So I leaned closer to the microphone and said, "I'm counting on all of you." I needed them to be my allies.

"You've earned this," Council president Bruce Harrell said, shaking my hand.

"Amen!" shouted the crowd.

## Meet My Sponsor

If somebody ever told me that one day I would be promoted to assistant chief, then deputy chief, and then selected chief of police, I would have encouraged them to go see a specialist, because clearly, they had lost their mind! Since day one, when I first heard that the police department was looking for new candidates while I was working at an insurance company, I had no idea that policing would become such an important part of my life. I know that, no matter what, I would have ended up being part of an organization or institution that catered to the community and strived for its betterment, because serving the people of Seattle has always been a source of great joy and pride to me. But deputy chief and then chief? It simply was not on my radar at the time.

So when then chief Kathleen O'Toole promoted me from assistant chief to deputy chief, I had to pick my jaw up off the floor. I was very honored and extremely surprised—floored. I spent the next three years working even harder, studying her leadership style, and attending meetings and conferences with her. But here's what I want to highlight: *she* was the one to bring me along to her meetings and conferences. She literally made sure I always had a seat at the table. Why? Because she knew that she was the first female chief of the Seattle Police Department, and she wanted to ensure she wouldn't be the last. She cared about the department and wanted to see qualified and experienced people being recognized for the value they brought to the department. She believed in me.

I still remember one of the first meetings she took me to. It was a rainy day in Seattle—to no one's surprise, of course—and temperatures were well below the seasonal average. Being late spring, windy and rainy days in the midforties were not the norm, thankfully. I was at the department as usual and Chief O'Toole called me into her office.

"You'll be coming with me to a conference next week," she said, nonchalantly.

"All right, thank you, Chief," I replied, trying to keep my composure as I still had to get used to going to meetings where most people outranked me. While I was confident of what I was capable of and what my worth in the department was, I also considered Chief O'Toole an incredibly inspiring person with a real aura about her, and I couldn't help feeling as though I still had my training wheels on when I was around her. As the conversation proceeded, she briefed me on what topics were going to be discussed and who was going to be there. I couldn't believe some of the names she said: it was like a glorified list of the who's who of law enforcement. My mouth went dry.

*This is big*, I thought to myself as I kept trying not to show that my heart was beating so fast that I felt as though I could feel my pulse in my neck.

On the day of the conference, I traveled with Chief O'Toole to the destination. We were in a rather large conference room at an elegant hotel in downtown Chicago, tables set up in a very large rectangle that could accommodate approximately seventy major city chiefs, a microphone in front of each seat. Blue-cushioned chairs lined three of the four sides of the table, and a pull-down projector screen embellished the fourth wall. As I stepped into the room, I could sense the experience, worth, and knowledge of those who were in attendance. I recognized many, and not because I had met them previously but because their reputations certainly preceded them as they were considered to be la crème de la crème in their field.

Darn it, my mouth was dry again.

"I'd like to introduce you to Deputy Chief Carmen Best," Chief O'Toole said, shocking me out of my daze and putting me on the spot all at once. "She's a rock star!"

I shook the hand of the person I was being introduced to and broadly smiled. Chief O'Toole's comment had made my whole day—no, scratch that; my whole year! And not because my head was suddenly too big for the building but because that comment translated into: "I see how hard you work and how much you care about the Seattle community, and I want to make sure other people—those who don't get to see the effort you put into your job every single day—are aware of it too." In one word, it was *validation*. When your boss takes the time out of a busy day to notice the performance of one employee, it means that your boss is somebody who truly cares about the workforce and the workplace.

"I would like to thank you for coming to . . ." the head of the conference began, inviting chiefs to introduce themselves as well as those they brought along with them—if any—before taking a seat so that discussions and presentations could be started.

After Chief O'Toole introduced me, I took a seat on one of the blue-cushioned chairs, along with the other deputy chiefs and plus-ones who had been lucky enough, like me, to be invited along.

"The agenda for today is going to include . . ." The speaker went on to list all the topics they were going to cover today—robberies, crimes, technology, and so forth.

Then, one by one, each chief made a presentation, some using the pull-down projector screen while others relied on the good ole "pass these copies around" method. Then, I saw Chief O'Toole stand up and walk toward me.

Did she forget something? I wondered. Maybe she needed a pen or a bottle of water or something.

"Carmen," she said, leaning closer to me and in a low tone so no one would hear her. "I have to take a call, so you have to cover for me while I'm gone."

Wha-what? I wanted to make sure I heard her correctly. "You want me to replace you at this meeting?"

"Yes, you're my deputy chief; it's part of your job," she said, straight to the point.

I gulped some air, my mouth drier than ever. I took a deep breath and walked toward the empty seat at the long rectangular table. I pulled out the chair and almost fell because my knees were weak. And my knees were weak because I was about to sit next to William Bratton, a highly respected law enforcement officer who served two terms as New York City police commissioner and had been Boston police commissioner as well as chief of police in Los Angeles. To say that I felt intimidated would be a huge understatement. After I somehow managed to sit down without making a fool of myself, I looked to my right and saw Bratton acknowledge my presence with a slight smile before he got back to focusing on the issue at hand.

*Oh my God, it's Bill Bratton!* I began coaching myself, *Carmen, do not say anything stupid. Don't you dare screw this up.*

"Does anybody want to share their view or opinion on the matter?" I heard the speaker say.

Wait, what matter? I had been so focused on not falling down or doing something to catch anybody's attention that I had completely lost mine and now had no clue what they had just finished discussing.

*Please don't ask me anything.* I suddenly felt like I was at a theater watching a performance when the presenter or actor or magician says, "Let's invite somebody from the audience onstage!" and the spotlight sweeps over each person in the audience and you're praying you quickly figure out how to be invisible, because you know you are going to mess it up while everybody's eyes are on you.

"Deputy Chief Best," the presenter said.

Lights on.

*Oh God . . . here we go.*

My time was up. I had to step up to the plate and show them my worth. I listened closely to the question they asked and answered it the best I could. When it was over, I looked over to my right again, and I saw that Bill Bratton had written something down on his notepad.

Uh-oh, did he take notes while I was speaking? I couldn't get myself to ask him, of course. He was too much of a celebrity to me, and I didn't want to unmask my inexperience or butcher my reputation, which had gotten a brand-new squeaky-clean makeover thanks to Chief O'Toole.

When the conference ended, I thanked Chief O'Toole for literally putting me at the table and revealed to her just how intimidated I had been of Bill Bratton.

"Did you talk to him though?"

"No, I was too tongue tied."

"Oh, you don't need to feel that way toward him. He's the most down-to-earth, humble person I have ever met. Have I told you how I started working with him?"

I shook my head no.

"I was probably thirty-one or thirty-two, and I had recently obtained my law degree when he tapped me on the shoulder and made me his assistant chief."

My lips slightly parted in fascination.

"He believed in me and put me on the map," she added. "He knew he was not going to be commissioner for the rest of his life, because at one point or another, he would leave the department. I think he really wanted to ensure that the hard work he had put into it wouldn't go to waste in the wrong hands. So he paid attention to those who worked with him and for him and carefully handpicked the ones he thought were better suited to take on such responsibility with honor and integrity. It's hard to find that person who, once put in a position of power, is not blinded by ego but is able to put it aside and focus on what's truly best for the community, you know? He guided me and coached me through it, making sure that I had a seat at the table, so to speak. He was truly my sponsor."

And that's when it clicked. That's when I realized she had done exactly the same with me, on that very day. She got up from her chair and allowed me to sit in it. By doing so, she made a big difference in my life because, through her, I learned what being a true leader really means.

## The Most Important Mentor, Ally, and Sponsor

I can't tell you how many times I have been asked: "Have you always wanted to become a police officer?" And the answer always makes me feel as though I let my audience down, because it is a straight, clear, and resounding *no*. I don't have a feel-good story of fulfilling my lifelong dream of becoming a police officer. So if that's the story you were expecting to read at some point in this book, I am sorry, it's not coming. But at least you are not alone in your expectation and disappointment—that I can guarantee you. So how did I start in the police force? Well, let's just say I didn't go out looking for the police force. On the contrary, it found me.

I remember this day as if it were yesterday. After the military, I began working at an insurance company and was in charge of doing accounts. I didn't know if that was what I wanted to do for the rest of my life, but I was in my early twenties and still trying to figure out where I belonged and what I was meant to do. Which is why, when I heard they were looking for police officers, I thought I might give it a try.

As I attended the police academy, I noticed just how many similarities there were with the military in terms of high expectations and regimen, and since I enjoyed my experience as a soldier, I felt confident I could stay and enjoy my time in the academy as well. My approach was, Well, let's just see what happens. As time went on, however, I kept overhearing people talk about me in rather derogatory terms.

"She's just too small to become a police officer," somebody said in hushed tones.

"I agree; she'll never make it out there being so petite," someone echoed.

"Well, she did pass the vocabulary test with 100 percent accuracy, so I guess she's not—"

"Shh! She's close by, she can hear you!"

Yep, I was close by. And I did hear. But what did I hear, exactly? I wasn't sure. Why were they fixating on my stature? Was it because I was a woman? I didn't think so because there were a few other women at the academy.

Was it because I was a Black person? I shook my head at that theory as well because there were a few other people of color there. Then why were they ganging up on me? I just couldn't put my finger on it. But I did hear their comments, and I heard them deep down in my soul. I knew I had to shake them off quickly before my inner being internalized their words—and then *that* was going to be real trouble. But I felt as though I just couldn't catch a break.

If the problem wasn't that I was a Black person, then the problem was that I was a woman. If the problem wasn't that I was a woman, then it was that I was the wrong kind of woman. I should not have been that petite and slender. According to their standards, I should have been bigger, perhaps with more meat on my bones, taller, and the list of the "right attributes" went on and on. When was it ever going to be enough? When was I ever going to be enough?

I sighed and walked away.

It didn't take long, however, for those hush-hush conversations to become more direct.

"Nah, you're too small to be a cop," one of my fellow academy recruits decided to voice to my face one day.

"Are you kidding me? You're so petite, you'll never be able to be a cop!" another one said, adding a juicy laugh, as if my stature was such a thigh slapper.

What was going on here?

I felt as though there was the police academy, with all its instructors and recruits, and then there was me. And it was open season: "See who can be the one to bring down Carmen Best."

But these people didn't know me. Sure, they saw I was a woman, a Black woman, a petite Black woman. But they didn't know I walked to school in the middle of a Pacific Northwest winter day with no gloves on when I was a child. They didn't know I wrote, edited, and rehearsed my student body president speech day and night until I felt it truly conveyed the message of unity that I wanted it to and believed it. They didn't know I congratulated my opponent when he won and offered to help him any way I could. They didn't know I trained hard to be on a highly successful track and field team in high school. They didn't know I trained and did push-ups on gravel in the Alabama heat. They didn't know I had been to Korea and Germany where I learned a whole lot about other cultures but so much more about myself. Simply put, they didn't know how resilient, determined, and driven I was.

I went to the bathroom, washed my face, and looked at myself in the tiny mirror in front of me. The person staring at me smiled with her eyes. I knew I had it in me to become a police officer—and a good one at that. I knew I was the right person for the job. And most of all, I knew I had a passion for serving my community. Yeah, I was petite. So what? I was petite when I joined the track and basketball teams as well. I was petite when I joined the military. But I still succeeded. My gender, race, and physical attributes had never stopped me before—I didn't let them. So why would I let them stop me now? Because a bunch of people had gathered in secret "let's bash Carmen" meetings? And because a few more had decided to voice their concerns about my career options right to my face? Oh, please. Who were *they* to judge? I took a deep breath, fixed my makeup, and walked out of the bathroom. Chin up, my steps paced and confident.

A few days later, we had a cumulative test on how to do a traffic stop. Most students went before me, but I was there watching everyone's performance—and also to see what to expect. It seemed pretty straightforward though: police officer stops car, walks to driver's side, asks for documents, and so on. Classic routine. Third student up, same thing happened. Seventh student up, same thing.

All right, nothing to write home about.

Then it was my turn.

It started as I expected: I got out of my police car and walked toward the car I had stopped—this was just a practice test, so people in the car were fellow academy recruits acting. I was about to approach the driver's side when, out of nowhere, the car wheeled away fast, screeching the tires.

*What the—!*

I ran back to my car, jumped in, and started to chase it—we were out in a field, not the actual street. Just as suddenly as the car had driven away, it stopped. I got out of my car as fast as I could when I saw somebody open the door of the passenger's side, jump out, and run away.

*What's happening?*

None of the other students had to deal with a car speeding off, then a passenger running away. Something was wrong here, but I couldn't dwell on it. I had a choice to make: chase the runaway or go to the driver's side and continue with the traffic stop. I had to think quickly on my feet and decided to continue with my traffic stop. So I walked to the driver's side and saw she had turned the ignition off and placed her hands on the steering wheel.

Okay, good.

"Your driver's license and registration," I said in a firm tone, trying hard not to convey just how confused I was about the outlandish chase and escape.

"Of course," she replied in a calm tone.

My heart rate slowed down a bit, finally. I felt beads of sweat collecting on my scalp, on my forehead. It wasn't a hot day in Seattle, and I was definitely not sweating from working out. This was clearly my body manifesting stress. I wanted to dry it off with my sleeve, but my instinct told me to keep a close eye on the driver. I had asked her to show me her documents, but she kept looking slightly to the passenger's seat—now empty.

*Why is she doing that?*

I couldn't figure it out. I was about to ask her for her license and registration again, when I saw it: a gun.

A gun? A gun!

I rushed to the passenger's side, opened the door, and grabbed the gun. I took it back to my car and secured it in my vehicle. Then, I walked back toward the driver and reapproached her.

"Ma'am, your driver's license and registration." The beads of sweat had suddenly turned icy hot.

"All right, you're done." I heard a voice in the background. I turned and saw our instructors there, arms crossed, lips tight. Then I saw the runaway walk back toward us, laughing out loud and complimenting himself for his performance, high-fiving other students along the way.

I stood there, watching the entire scene unfold. Then I saw the female driver walk back toward me.

"I have never seen anything like that," she whispered, standing close to me.

I knew she was referring to the many unexpected twists that happened during my traffic stop test. Nobody before me or after me had to deal with any of these extra scenarios. I was the lucky one, I guess.

"I'm sure," I said and walked away.

Eventually, I was told I had passed the test and graduated from the police academy. But I knew that nobody was happy about that—nobody but me, of course. I think I was tested and judged more harshly than others.

Had I allowed them to truly get to me, I wouldn't have written this book as there wouldn't have been Chief Carmen Best. But I didn't let them. I knew who I was, and I knew what I was capable of doing. I knew my values and what I stood for. And I knew what I didn't tolerate. It was during my time at the academy that, with each challenge, insult, and obstacle they threw at me, I learned my most valuable lesson of all: I am and will always have to be my most important mentor, ally, and sponsor.

# TACTICAL DEBRIEF

**THERE ARE PEOPLE** you will encounter throughout your career who will willingly become your mentors, allies, and sponsors. You won't have to ask them to take on that role; they will do it voluntarily. And when they do, be sure to check your ego at the door and listen, because remember: you don't know it all. Your mentors, allies, and sponsors will be there to guide you, support you, and ensure that you, too, have a seat at the table. And when you become more experienced and feel qualified enough, look at the newcomers and identify hard work, commitment, and integrity. Once you do, become that newcomer's mentor or ally or sponsor. You won't be the last CEO, doctor, or senior editor. You must ensure there is continuity within the department, organization, or company. And the only way to do it is by investing time in new generations and sharing with them your knowledge and lessons learned through the hard school of experience.

But before we conclude, I want you to remember one thing: before my mentor Sergeant Patricia Hayes, before my law enforcement and community allies, and before my sponsor Kathleen O'Toole, there was the most important mentor, ally, and sponsor of all, without whom I would have had no need for any of the ones previously listed: me.

1.  Can you think of a time when you were the only one to believe in yourself, so much so that you proved everyone else wrong?
2.  Which person has taken on the role of mentor or sponsor in your life or career?
3.  Think of the people you have met throughout your life and the relationships you've established with them: who would you consider your allies?
4.  Have you ever been a mentor, ally, or sponsor? If so, what are qualities you looked for in your protégé that convinced you they were worth your support?

# 4

# The Challenges of Situational Leadership

Leadership is a skill set acquired over time. But it is not the most important skill set. You see, your leadership skills in general will allow you to sit in the big chair, so to speak, but they won't keep you there for long unless you are able to develop the one skill that has failed many leaders: situational leadership. To put it simply, situational leadership is the ability to adapt your leadership style to the matter at hand and the skill sets of those involved, often requiring you to think quickly on your feet.

After then chief Kathleen O'Toole chose me to be her second-in-command by promoting me to deputy chief, I spent my time dealing with matters I believed to be some of the most challenging I could have ever experienced. From pushing the federal consent decree forward and responding to major incidents, to monitoring the budget and managing the interpersonal issues, I learned a lot. It was tiring and stressful but also meaningful and fulfilling because not only was I serving my community in a different capacity, I knew that I was acquiring leadership skills I needed to improve and become better at what I was entrusted with. Yet nothing could have prepared me for what I was going to face years later.

When I became chief, I was determined to implement the lessons I had learned throughout my career. At the top of my priorities was to ensure that the command staff remained as diverse as possible, with different people bringing different ideas and experiences into the room. After doing so, it was time for me to work with my team members—because for any organization to succeed, it needs to address problems with the right approach to identifying the causes, the right approach to using data, and the right approach to consulting people. You have to set that stage, which means that, at the beginning, you have to get into the weeds—or what some call micromanaging.

When you feel confident that your team has absorbed your leadership style and requirements, it is time for you to take a step back and put them to the test. For example, I began asking my team questions about how they would handle certain situations or what they would do in this or that scenario. Based on the answers they developed, I knew if they were ready to be given more responsibilities and latitude in decision-making, or if they needed a bit more time. Of course, this approach assumes that you do have time to let the team practice. If you are in a highly operational organization, this might not be a reality for you. If so, you'll benefit from the leadership lesson I am about to share. I consider myself lucky because I had a good eighteen months or so before a true crisis hit. And that's when I faced some of the most challenging situational leadership tests of my entire career.

## The Most Challenging Year

When I welcomed the New Year on January 1, 2020, I had no idea of the many unprecedented situational leadership tests I would have to face within a matter of days. These challenges would put my leadership skills to the test, force me to confront difficult tasks, and ensure that I supported those around me to help them build confidence in their leadership capabilities. Looking back now, I shake my head and sigh at all that happened and how unaware I was of what was to come after New Year's. And how could I have known? After all, the year had started just like any other . . .

Much like the rest of the world, Seattle woke up to a brand-new decade. Every new beginning represents a chance for people to reflect upon what has been done so far, weigh the good and the bad, identify areas that need improvement, and vow to keep doing their best. The media highlighted the decade in review, captured people across the world offering their most genuine and festive smiles as fireworks embellished the background, and proposed a to-do list for those in charge of the country's safety and progress.

I woke up that morning and smiled. *Good morning to you, 2020!* As I put my uniform on, I thought of my beautiful and talented daughters, who had grown up so much and so fast, becoming contributing members to society and carrying on with grace and determination. I thought of my family, who had been living in the Seattle area for five generations, many of whom had dedicated their lives to its betterment. I thought of my officers and all of the employees, those who celebrated the New Year at home with their families and those who stayed at work to ensure public safety. I thought of my community: the teachers who would soon welcome students back to school to guide and coach the brilliant minds of tomorrow; the hairdressers who would allow women and men to sit back and relax while in their care and give them a boost of confidence with their new do; the bakers whose scrumptious desserts and pastries would bring a smile to their customers' faces and be the centerpiece of friendly conversations and get-togethers; and the hospital workers who would tend to their patients with tact and care, ensuring their recovery and helping ease their pain.

In that moment, as I walked out the door to head to work, I felt immensely proud of the city I had worked in and supported for most of my life. But I knew that we still had a lot to do to improve. We faced complex social issues we needed to address as soon as possible. Our homeless population had been increasing, with Seattle ranking third in the country—after New York City and Los Angeles. Racial disparities in the criminal justice system were still very much a painful reality—one I was determined to tackle head-on. Drug and alcohol addiction had also been on the rise, with teenagers becoming more and more involved in illicit substances. To the surprise of no one, the increasing use of drugs and alcohol—especially among the youth—was a symptom of a much more dangerous problem: mental illness. Depression was rampant among teenagers in Washington State, and reports of self-harm and suicidal thoughts had come in at a much higher rate than the national average. Clearly, we still had a lot of work ahead of us.

The month of January was going to start with a trip abroad for me. I was scheduled to go to Qatar—a country I had never been to but had always wanted to go visit—as part of a law enforcement exchange program with Seattle Pacific University. I had put a lot of work into my speech and was happy with the result: some things never change; I was still the girl who ran for student body president! As we got closer to my departure date, however, the mayor decided it was best for me not to go, and I accepted her decision, choosing my deputy chief to go on my behalf. And thank goodness I didn't go. In a matter of days, Seattle would be making headlines across the world.


WEDNESDAY, JANUARY 22, 2020

The sky was gloomy, and the air made you shiver from the inside out. The high was supposed to be fifty-three degrees, with a low of forty-two—pretty average for Seattle, yet it was still one of those days that, just by looking at it, made you go, "Ugh." I was on call that day. We had officers going to do a buy-bust operation—which means they were locating two suspected drug dealers—in downtown Seattle, on the corner of the Pike and Pine corridor, between Fourth and Second Avenues. The area had already been the site of a shooting the day before, where a man in his fifties was found injured with a gunshot wound in a stairwell at the mall on the 1600 block of Fourth Avenue. Unfortunately, the man died three hours after being transported to Harborview Medical Center.

"Officer-involved shooting in Belltown area" was the message delivered to me at around three in the afternoon. I immediately went downtown with a member of my command staff to evaluate the situation, talk to the officers, figure out the scenario, and follow our normal protocol of having an independent agency come to the area and carry out a review. This latest step was one of many grassroot initiatives aimed at addressing localized problems. Once there, I was informed that the suspect, a twenty-five-year-old man, had rammed a patrol car. When the officers attempted to make an arrest, they saw the man was armed. Then, he confronted one of the officers, who responded. The suspect was struck by gunfire but was not dead. When captured, he was given a service blanket, because he was shirtless, and was taken to Harborview for evaluation and to treat his injuries, which were not life threatening. After a couple of hours, the situation was resolved, and we headed back to headquarters.

"Shots fired downtown on Third Avenue," I heard on the call.

*Wait, what?*

It felt like déjà vu. It was now five in the afternoon, and we were still downtown. We immediately turned around and went back to the area, which was quite chaotic. People running away from the scene, police cars everywhere, lots of screaming and shouting. We didn't have many details as to what had happened: Was it a lone shooter? Was it an active shooter? Was it domestic terrorism?

We began canvassing for witnesses and information and soon learned that there had been a dispute between suspected drug dealers outside a McDonald's. The drug deal had clearly gone awry, and they had started shooting indiscriminately at each other, ultimately hitting eight people.

One of them was a nine-year-old boy who was shot in the abdomen. He was on a trip to the Seattle Aquarium, with his family. Since opening in 1977, the aquarium has been a source of pride for the Seattle area and a great way to combine education and fun.

The boy was on the sidewalk, walking toward one of the many restaurants and food joints lined up on Third Avenue with others looking to grab a bite to eat. When the police officers and fire department personnel arrived and began to triage victims and treat people, the boy told them not to worry about him because there were other people injured.

"Please make sure you take care of them," he said, holding onto his abdomen. "I am going to be fine, don't worry."

When I heard what he said, my heart felt heavy, and time slowed down. I was suddenly transported back to when my own daughters were his age. They, too, had gone on field trips to the aquarium. They, too, had eaten at some of the local restaurants as a fun treat for the day. I could see their faces in this little boy's face, and it felt as though the air had been punched out of my lungs. First responders moved quickly to transport him and other victims to Harborview. Two women died from their injuries. Two Amazon employees, who just happened to step outside of the Amazon building as they would on any workday, were shot as well.

After the area had been secured and access restricted with yellow and red tape, the team started locating buses in the area and pulled surveillance video from them, as well as from nearby stores, to gather as much information as possible. Meanwhile, we were providing information to city hall and the deputy mayor—the mayor was out of town at that point. We deployed our homicide unit and gang unit—which is a police detective unit tasked with doing proactive work with people who often engage or are ancillary to these types of criminal activities. Witnesses said that they heard shots fired and saw people running for cover or drop to the ground. A man who was shot in the leg collapsed to the ground, a nearby café locked its doors while the customers inside sought shelter behind the register and underneath the tables. Within a one-block radius, people sobbed, others screamed, others stood silent in a daze, eyes wide open, staring into nothing.

This particular area of Seattle was not new to violence, but this was one of the worst mass shootings we had ever witnessed—especially coming on the heels of two other shootings within twenty-four hours. The community had often expressed their concerns over the drug trafficking problems on Third Avenue, and now they were even more concerned. Angst and fear had increased in both residents and business owners—understandably so, I might add. Reporters from various media outlets had arrived on the scene as well, and fire department chief Harold Scoggins and I were releasing statements to the press to keep them—and the public—informed as to what was happening and what we were able to determine as we processed the scene and information came forward. We also released information about the suspects, and one of our former gang detectives quickly recognized one of them, thus allowing us to identify him as well as the other suspect—even though they remained at large.

Later that night, at home, I fell onto the couch and closed my eyes. All I could see was the crime scene: a body on the ground covered by a sheet, people with their hands on their head in despair, the flashing lights of law enforcement vehicles with loud sirens on. The boy's voice echoed in my head. A day that was supposed to be a whole lot of fun for him in the big city, exploring the aquarium, eating at fun places, turned into a tragedy he will never forget. My stomach hurt in disgust. I sighed heavily. Things had to change. And fast.

The day after, I spoke with the mayor and told her that we needed to go to Amazon and talk to the employees in an attempt to transparently address their fears and concerns, because nobody should go to work fearing that they or their colleagues would walk out the door and get struck by a bullet. Afterward, I went to the Downtown Seattle Association and talked to the local business owners, trying to reassure them as well that the Seattle police was going to take important steps to ensure public safety and take care of the many issues that had been afflicting that specific area. One solution my team and I came up with was to have officers in uniform standing there every day, every shift, day and night. I, myself, drove down there at least twice a day just to see what was happening and to make sure all was well and under control. We hoped that the uniformed presence would deter people with ill intentions.

A few days after the mass shooting, we located the suspects. We had been working closely with our federal partners—the Federal Bureau of Investigation; the Bureau of Alcohol, Tobacco, Firearms and Explosives; the Drug Enforcement Administration; and the US Marshals. It was the Marshal Service that found the two suspects: they were in Las Vegas. They quickly arrested them and brought them into custody, to the relief of many—me included. That night I slept well, comforted by the thought that those who had caused so much harm and pain were finally where they belonged. Little did I know that it would be a long, long time before I got a good night's sleep again.

MONDAY, FEBRUARY 24, 2020

They say that when it rains, it pours, right? Well, it must be true, because around the same day as the mass shooting in Seattle, Washington State reported its first confirmed case of coronavirus. To make things worse, it was the first confirmed case in the whole country. Suddenly, the state I called home was ground zero. We already had the eyes of the world on us because of the recent gun violence. Now we were making headlines because of this scary virus that had been claiming many victims over the past month in Asia. To say that people were afraid would be an understatement. We were terrified! What was this virus? What were the symptoms? Who was most at risk? What precautions were we supposed to take? So many questions, yet no answers. And we had no time to sit and think either. Roughly a month after the first case in the state, Seattle reported its first community-transmitted case in the city. It was time to act.

We knew that we would probably be considered essential workers, but people didn't want to go out. What did it mean for the health of the officers? Who had preexisting or compromised health conditions? And what about the protective equipment? If we had a COVID-positive employee—which we did—what was expected of us? Were they to be quarantined? Were they to be isolated? How long did they isolate for? How long did they quarantine for? How did we test? None of that had been established yet.

Fortunately for us, city employees stepped up. They set up the Emergency Operations Center—from which all of the various city departments and their responses were managed. They were also coordinating with Dr. Jeffrey Duchin—an epidemiology expert—and other public health doctors, spokespersons, the Centers for

Disease Control and Prevention, and the World Health Organization, pulling together all the necessary information so that we could have an appropriate response. Yes, we had previously dealt with other dangerous viruses, like H1N1. But COVID-19 was a whole other beast.

One of the first things we were instructed to do was to outfit all of our officers with personal protective equipment (PPE). As instructions were provided, we noticed that there was conflicting information coming from the health department and the CDC—they weren't always in sync. More questions were raised on the verbiage and definitions related to the virus and our response: Who was considered to be an essential worker? What were the rules about social distancing? Once we were told that we had to be within six feet of one another for more than ten minutes for it to be considered an exposure, we had even more doubts about definitions and measures: What was an exposure? Was it an incident? What were we protecting for? How would we monitor?

The government relied on the REDCap system, which had been created at Vanderbilt University in Nashville, Tennessee, in 2004, and was used to support a small number of clinical researchers who needed to collect data in safety and in compliance with patient privacy laws. Thanks to this system, people in our county were able to connect to health-care professionals online twenty-four hours a day and relate their symptoms or share if they had been exposed to the virus. Once all the necessary information had been gathered, the health-care professionals instructed patients to isolate or quarantine for a certain number of days—some said a week, others said ten days, others said fourteen days; given how new the situation was, even health-care professionals didn't know what to recommend.

Soon after, we created one of the first testing sites for COVID-19. To do so, we had to contract with the hospital and with the University of Washington. We set up the testing site in a big open area, where cars could drive through. The Seattle Police Department and the Seattle Fire Department had been trained to perform the test swabs as instructed by Dr. Duchin. Once the patient had been swabbed, we would have to put the test in the vial, seal the vial, mark it, and put it in a large cooler. Every day, we would transport the cooler to the University of Washington Research, where they would analyze the test swabs right away, and after roughly forty-eight hours, people would receive the results. It took a lot of coordination to make it all happen.

I was truly thrilled with my team who, from morning to night, worked tirelessly to figure things out, answer questions, make calls with other city departments, and so much more. This was a time of unprecedented crisis, where our state was the first to face an invisible enemy that we knew was a threat but didn't know where it was, when it would hit, or how to protect ourselves against it. We didn't even know that we were dealing with a pandemic yet—for most of us, a pandemic was something we had only read about in history books, never thinking it would be a reality we would have to face in the twenty-first century.

But it was during such a time of crisis that everybody on my team stepped up and shined. I was super proud of my staff and realized that some of the folks went above and beyond to help and ensure we had a good handle on whatever was going on. There was so much work to get done that days quickly turned into late afternoons, and late afternoons quickly turned into nights. We were often at work past nine or ten at night. Yet, nobody complained. I gained a whole new level of respect for my team—not that I didn't appreciate my whole team before the pandemic. But I saw what they really could do, and I believe it was a huge boost of self-confidence for them as well.

In a time when the whole world was holding its breath and shaking every time there was a new positive case to add to the ever-expanding list of coronavirus-affected patients, everyone at the Seattle Police Department made themselves available by being proactive and productive. I cherished and looked forward to our morning meetings during which we walked through everything that happened overnight, what our plans were for the day, and what we were doing. Then we would break and do all the work we set out to do. At around five, we would regroup to discuss what happened during the day and what else was on for the night. It was a period of growth and team building.

While everybody worked so hard, one person stood out for me, and that was Mike Fields, our HR director. He was working every single day—we were pulling eighteen-hour days. He was coordinating with all the people, setting up the rules, the guidelines, the liability, the structure, talking to the union, coordinating with them, helping them understand what to do and how we were working to protect employees and specifically their membership. There was a lot to it, and he was working those long hours getting it done. Two weeks later, once we had all systems in place, I went to see him and said, "I don't want you to do anything this weekend. Go home, rest, do not come to work."

He looked at me, puzzled.

"You agree?"

"Okay," he said, thanking me with a smile.

The next day, a Saturday, I went into work expecting not to see him because it was supposed to be his first day off. I opened the door to the office and there he was.

"I thought you were supposed to be home!" I said in a tone that conveyed just how surprised I was to see him. I knew he was committed to helping out. And I couldn't have been more grateful. It was thanks to people like Mike, who worked tirelessly behind the scenes to ensure public safety, that I felt a little less worried about this unprecedented situation we found ourselves in.

At the same time, however, my heart was aching. I was worried for my daughters, who, though young and healthy, were at risk of being exposed each day because of what they did for a living. I was worried about my officers and their family members. I was worried about my community: the many teachers who suddenly had to switch to online schooling and learn to handle a brand-new way of performing their job within a matter of days; the many hairdressers and bakers who had to shut down their businesses because of lockdown; the many essential workers who were suddenly faced with an invisible yet deadly virus and had to stare death in the face every single day.

More often than not, at the end of every workday, I was just too exhausted to even go back home, so I slept at work, fearing that another emergency might come up out of nowhere and wanting to be ready. Meanwhile, the media were reporting false information about me, claiming that I was going to abandon the Seattle Police Department to go look for another chief job somewhere else, accusing me of spending more time away from Seattle than at work. Normally, I would not give in to idle gossiping, but this one hit home for me because I didn't want my team and community to believe such accusations. I also knew the world was watching, and I felt compelled to set things straight. So I released an official statement to my fellow officers:

In the Editor's Notes column of The Guardian, there are several claims that are false. Because false information unchecked will soon take on a life of its own, I am writing to address two key points in immediate need of correction.

### I AM NOT A CANDIDATE FOR ANOTHER POLICE CHIEF JOB, NOR AM I SEEKING ONE OUT

It is an honor for me to serve as your Chief, and I competed for the opportunity. This is my department. I spent my entire career here, growing professionally alongside many of you.

### LEADING OUR DEPARTMENT

I lead from the front. Whether it's a significant scene of violence, or a foot beat at 3rd and Pine, you've seen me there.

To say that I am out of town attending conferences and seminars more than I am here is just plain ridiculous. Every one of you is working hard. I see how committed the men and women of our department are to our city, and I recognize your work at every opportunity. Business travel is part of my job. Recruiting and retention, officer wellness, the fentanyl epidemic, and homelessness are national police issues. We benefit by working with other departments across the country to develop strategies that make our officers safer and our department stronger.

## OUR DEPARTMENT IS A NATIONAL MODEL FOR POLICING

Other departments send personnel to our department to learn about our response to bias crimes, crowd management, crisis intervention, and tactical de-escalation. All of this is true—not just because we've done the work in our city, but because we showcased our success to our counterparts across our profession.

We're all in this together. Whether working through COVID-19 or filling our chairs at the academy with SPD recruits, we will only succeed by supporting one another, not by tearing each other down.

We joined this profession to support public safety. We knew it was going to be a hard job, but we have the best men and women in the country working here. It is an honor to serve as your Chief, and I couldn't be more proud to be a part of this organization.

There is no greater city, and no greater calling. Take care of one another and be safe out there.[1]

As days turned into weeks and weeks turned into months, the coronavirus was finally declared a pandemic. We helplessly watched the world mourn and witnessed the coming together of people from different walks of life displaying three of the most important attributes I had first noticed in my team's response to the crisis: resiliency, hope, and courage. Young children in Canada, the United Kingdom, the United States, and many other countries began drawing rainbows and posting their drawings on windows as a way to spread cheer and feel less isolated in a world that had suddenly turned our lives upside down; people in Italy stepped outside their balconies and sang in unison; the brightest minds of many different countries gathered to hopefully find a vaccine for this virus and save as many lives as possible.

Every day I put on my uniform and walked into the department, I was reminded of how invaluable my whole team was in establishing COVID-19 protocols not just for our county and state, but for the whole nation. I was proud of the way Seattle rose to the occasion and became a beacon of hope and light in what was one of the most challenging situational leadership tests that I, our police department, city, state, and country have ever had to face. And then, it all changed again.

MONDAY, MAY 25, 2020

An African American man in his midforties named George Floyd was in a convenience store to buy cigarettes in Minneapolis, Minnesota. The store clerk believed Floyd used a counterfeit twenty-dollar bill and called 911 to report the crime. Within seventeen minutes from the moment the first patrol car showed up at the convenience store, Floyd was pinned down to the ground by three officers. One police officer pressed his knee into Floyd's neck for more than nine minutes, killing him.

Bystanders captured his last few moments of life on video, which was quickly shared on social media and seen all over the world. He was heard saying "I can't breathe" and calling for his mother. As a Black woman and mother, that video hit me right through my soul. My heart ached in so many ways. As a police chief— who clearly supported the profession in many ways but knew that we had often been on the wrong side of good—I was outraged. People were angry, and I recognized and understood that anger. I empathized and comprehended.

I kept going back to that police officer who killed Floyd and thought to myself, *On both a policing and human level, how could you do that and be okay with it?* I kept hearing people question whether that was part of his training, and all I wanted to do was scream "Does it matter?" He was a human being kneeling on another human being's neck, suffocating him and eventually killing him. It was inexcusable! I wanted the Seattle Police Department to know where I stood and what I expected of them. So I felt compelled to release a statement to my officers right away:

I wanted to take a moment to address the tragic murder of George Floyd by the Minneapolis Police Department officer.

In the video, we hear Mr. Floyd's repeated calls for help. We hear him say over and over again that he cannot breathe.

The video is upsetting, disappointing, and infuriating. It does not show the policing we know. Policing is an honorable profession filled with honorable public servants. We are committed to protecting life and serving the community.

Because of the Seattle Police Department's high level of training, our commitment to de-escalation, and our track record of limiting the use of force, I have confidence that something like this would not occur in our city.

Especially troubling about the video, was the officers who stood by while Mr. Floyd called for help.

As a police officer, you have a sworn duty to uphold the law and do what is right. We prioritize the sanctity of life in every situation.

If you see a co-worker doing something that is unsafe, out of policy, unacceptable, or illegal, you need to act. This goes beyond reporting. If someone's life is unnecessarily in danger, it is your responsibility to intervene.

We each have a right to go home at the end of the day, but we also have a responsibility to ensure that others enjoy that same right. We must hold ourselves accountable if we are to maintain the trust of the community who grants us the privilege to serve them.

I know it can be challenging to see these incidents, even when they do not happen here. You all should be proud of how we provide police services here in Seattle.

Thank you for all that you do, every day. Stay safe.[2]

The day after Floyd's death, protests erupted in Minneapolis. Then, like wildfire, they spread throughout the country. Seattle was no exception. We knew there were going to be significant numbers of people coming to protest because they were retraumatized by the event—I say retraumatized because this was not the first case of a White police officer killing an African American man or woman and not the first case of police brutality; history tends to repeat itself if we don't learn from it, and, clearly, we have yet to learn.

We also knew there would be a coming together of Black Lives Matter. What we didn't know, however, was how a protest would function during current safety issues concerning the pandemic. Restaurants and other businesses were closed. Children were not in school. Theaters and other entertainment venues were not available. Clearly, people had a lot of free time on their hands—they could protest for weeks if they really wanted to—and they could show up by the thousands.

"Tonight, they are going to Chinatown-International District to create mayhem," one of the officers reported.

It was Friday, May 29, and we had a plan for what was to come. But when we looked around, we didn't really see anything. Our plans were not set in stone because we needed to be prepared for almost anything, given these new and unprecedented times with COVID-19. It was unclear how many officers we would need and which groups might show up. We weren't sure what exactly to be ready for, but we were on alert and ready to act, if needed. We were as prepared as we could be but knew we might need to change direction as events unfolded.

Then, at around seven in the evening, a very organized crowd of about 150 people showed up dressed primarily in black in Chinatown-International District, jumped out of parked cars all at once—some were on bicycles—had a rally, and drove the wrong way heading northbound on Fifth Avenue chanting: "George Floyd!" "I can't breathe!" and "Stop killing us!"

We did not have enough officers to address that group because they had showed up unexpectedly. Immediately, we called in officers from home. I was so thankful to see that they all picked up the phone and came downtown.

Once at the precinct, they had to change into their protective gear and get ready for what was to come. Obviously, as fast as our officers responded from home and elsewhere, protesters still had a leg up. Our bicycle officers arrived to help minimize any potential negative impact—Black Bloc members have been described as anarchists who, from my experience, often conceal their identity and protest in violent ways.

I was sitting in my office and saw them coming up the street, weaving in and out of cars and going the opposite direction of traffic flow. The protesters pointed green lasers at the officers. They threw fireworks and hurled debris toward the officers. Many of them began damaging property, breaking the windows of local stores.

Police did their best to push back the crowd by using pepper spray, but the protesters soon dispersed into several, smaller groups and traipsed around the city. By eleven, most of the protesters had dissipated, but a group of about fifty remained around Fifth Avenue under the officers' close watch. The protest went well into the early hours of Saturday morning and police made several arrests. I took a deep breath when I saw that we had no injuries among officers and protesters. Day one, down. Time to get ready for day two.

**THAT FRIDAY, I** had to undergo a minor procedure, and after getting it done, I went back to work even though I wasn't feeling my best. Still, I knew more protests were planned. We had an Incident Action Plan (IAP) set up, and I wanted to ensure I was on-site and engaged, because I didn't want to leave our officers alone. The IAP is a situationally based plan that states the commander's intent—meaning, what they want to see happen and how—roll call times, locations, who's working what post, legal authority issues, briefing materials, weather forecasts, medic units on scene, and much more.

Our plan that day was simple and effective: all hands on deck. We had several platoons deployed. I had left the incident commander in charge. Along with my deputy chief, I went to the Seattle police operation center—the hub where all the operations were occurring, where decisions were being made, and where people were being deployed from, and so on. I walked down the hall toward the two rooms we operated from: one room had people from other agencies whom we were coordinating with; the other was a smaller conference room we normally used to discuss our plan and figure out what the action was going to be like. I knew my deputy and I would find the commander in the conference room. What I didn't know, however, was that he was all we would find: he was the only person in the room, which was truly odd.

"Where is everybody?" I asked him as soon as I stepped into the room. My higher-than-normal tone conveyed just how surprised I was to find him alone.

"Oh, they're all out there. Let me call in."

I clenched my teeth.

"What do you mean, 'Let me call in'?" My tone was even higher now. I knew things were happening quickly and the temperature was heating up in the field. I needed him to brief me on what was going on, what operations were been carried out, and so on.

"What's our game plan? How are people deployed? What is our next operational period? What is our plan moving down the line? Who are we talking to or coordinating with?" I threw questions at him, hoping he had at least one answer.

But no such luck. The deputy chief and I shared a quiet look of concern.

There, in front of me, was a situational leadership test: the person I had left in charge to lead the mission seemed to be struggling. So I now faced a situation I did not anticipate, and I had two choices: one, keep bombarding him with questions and perhaps throw a lecture in there as well for good measure; two, adapt to the situation quickly and take charge.

I looked at my deputy chief and said, "Take the green marker. I'll take the orange one." I instructed him as I pointed to the whiteboard in front of us. "Let's start writing."

"Platoon One: Mission? Location?" I wrote. We needed details so we could follow the operation. "Call them now and get the information," I told him.

A minute or so later, he came back to the conference room and said, "I called in and I know each one of the lieutenants is out in the field; they've all answered."

*What?!*

We had prepared him and worked with him, and as I understood what was happening (or wasn't happening), we jumped in to help and eventually took over.

Another situational leadership test: taking the lead and guiding him through the process was not working as quickly as I needed it to. We couldn't build the plane while we were flying it, basically. So I had two options again: keep getting mad or call for backup.

I called others in to help. Then, I let him know that we would circle back later with him. We needed to get this situation under control. I could tell he wanted to stay and help. He was a hard worker, committed to his service to the community.

But there was no time to keep dwelling on the situation. There was an active protest going on, and we had to get a hold of it. There were two different groups of protesters: one was rallying up toward Seattle Police Headquarters on Fifth Avenue, while the other was with several ministers rallying at Westlake Center—right in the heart of downtown. Both groups combined, we estimated there were roughly fifteen thousand protesters. Our police force had fourteen hundred members. You do the math.

Among the protesters, most people just came to listen to the speeches, to show their solidarity with Black Lives Matter, to lament what happened to George Floyd, and to demonstrate against police brutality. Members of my own family were among the peaceful protesters, and had I not been working that day, I would have certainly joined them—over the upcoming months, I did eventually join a Black Lives Matter demonstration in support of the movement. Many of them marched with their hands up chanting, "Hands up, don't shoot!" and "What's his name? George Floyd!" Meanwhile, the pandemic was very much rampant, and we were concerned about so few people wearing masks or social distancing. Seattle city workers quickly prepared to hand out hundreds of single-use masks, water, and sanitizing wipes to demonstrators in need.

But there were also people who were up to no good, and we had to prepare to face them and ensure public safety. What started as a peaceful protest soon went awry. Within a matter of hours, things escalated, and the situation became extremely dangerous. Vehicles were set on fire, there was lots of looting, businesses were severely damaged, people were injured. Elderly residents of high-rise buildings called 911, saying, "We feel trapped!" They were becoming increasingly worried that, due to the many fires set on their streets, the elevators would be shut down and, given their age, they would not be able to get down more than fourteen flights of stairs.

As tensions grew, police officers began using bikes and pepper spray to contain the crowds of unruly demonstrators. Protesters also walked on Interstate 5, which was quickly closed to traffic in both directions between I-90 and Highway 520 to avoid a tragedy. Acts of vandalism continued, and graffiti with threats to the police was sprayed across many buildings. Crowds were quickly moving up to Eleventh Avenue, getting closer and closer to the East Precinct. They were getting wilder and more dangerous as they started throwing bottles and rocks at our officers, who were running short on the nonlethal tools they needed to defend themselves and community members, such as pepper spray and blast balls.

At one point, someone drove a car through the crowd near the precinct, jumped out with a gun, and fired a shot. He was immediately taken into custody, but we were certainly not in the clear. I instructed the officers to issue a dispersal order to the crowds. When we saw the crowds ignore the order, the officers gave warnings to disperse. Still nothing. At that point, I had no choice but to approve the use of tear gas. While I dreaded the decision, from my years of law enforcement experience, I knew this was the only way to avoid a tragedy.

The protests did not die down. Rather, they intensified. And people began asking me if we were going to deploy the National Guard. To them, it seemed like the next reasonable step because it was clear that we were outnumbered and needed to get the protests under control to ensure public safety. To me, this was not an easy decision to make. Why? Because I looked past the uniform.

Have you ever done that before? As I thought of calling in the National Guard, I couldn't help thinking that these military members were somebody's children in their early twenties, many the same age as my own daughters. And my call would have made them put their lives at risk. But we were facing a serious threat to public safety, and it was truly the best option. But I was also aware that some protesters would see this move as an act of aggression rather than defense, which would put these troops at risk of being on the receiving end of violence.

As much as I wanted to, I knew I didn't have time to dwell on it. I had a situational leadership test to face: Call in the National Guard to help my officers keep the protest safe or avoid putting these young people at risk?

"Call them in," I said. "But they won't be armed. If the protesters see the National Guard armed, they will take it the wrong way and fear we are going to attack them. That's not what we want. We want them to feel protected as they exercise their constitutional right." The National Guard turned out to be invaluable to us, especially when it came to protecting the precinct. Late into Saturday night—actually, more like early Sunday morning—I gathered them all at headquarters and thanked them for their selfless service. "You defended the 1519 today and should be incredibly proud of yourselves," I began, referring to the address of the East Precinct—1519 Twelfth Avenue. "Without you, the city of Seattle would be in grave danger still, so I applaud you all for your support and courage."

Then, it was time to address the department, the press, and the citizens. So I released another statement:

I want to update you on events of today and tonight. Currently, we are still addressing a number of groups of offenders who continue to assault officers and loot the downtown core, indiscriminately. The National Guard is assisting in controlling the situation downtown. At last update we had arrested 27 individuals for a variety of offenses from assault, to arson, to destruction and looting. The priority is protecting life and ending the destruction. At this moment we know multiple officers and civilians have been injured. The Seattle Police Department was prepared to facilitate the peaceful exercise of First Amendment rights. In the aftermath of the murder of George Floyd we all are rightfully angry, sad, frustrated, and heartbroken. Due to the actions of some groups who wanted to take advantage of this situation—what started peacefully around Noon, became violent and destructive around 2:40pm. At that time, officers began being assaulted with rocks, bottles, and other projectiles. At 2:38pm the first dispersal order was issued as the demonstration became unlawful and then a riot. Offenders were throwing and using incendiary devices including Molotov cocktails. These devices quickly ignited several city and private vehicles.

As the situation continued to intensify, protestors entered the freeway at Spring St and attacked government buildings. As these groups refused to listen to commands or stop their destruction, SPD officers then had to deploy crowd control measures to end the lawlessness as assaults on officers and property continued. At no time have officers discharged their firearms. There were countless uses of non-lethal and crowd control tools. Protestors then started looting businesses. SPD asked, in addition to the significant number of planned mutual aid resources that had already been planned, for additional mutual aid, including National Guard resources.

At 5pm, the Mayor declared a citywide curfew from 5pm to 5am. This gave officers additional tools to disperse crowds, but the priority remains addressing violent crime and destruction by offenders already disobeying dispersal orders. We are

planning for the rest of the night and tomorrow. We will continue to respond swiftly to all acts of violence and destruction.
I want to commend all of the officers, from Seattle and our
mutual aid partners, for their tireless work today to protect
this city.[3]

At around two in the morning, I went outside to assess the damage and see what was happening. The
crowd had dissipated for the most part, but the thousand or so people left were the most dangerous and
aggressive.

"Just so you know, they are still throwing lots of stuff
at us," I told the mayor when I called her around three
in the morning to update her. There seemed to be no
end in sight.

The protests went on, and we had more work to do.
We eventually coordinated with the Office of the In-
spector General, the Office of Police Accountability,
and the Community Police Commission to do an analysis and review of all the events. Simultaneously, we had
asked the Center for Policing Equity to do an independent review about what happened, the decision-making
process, and give us some recommendations. Then I,
myself, went to the International Association of Chiefs
of Police and asked if I could have some help coordinating a meeting to discuss how we might respond to
these situations better. We had to evolve our approach
of dispersing the crowds because, clearly, our current
approach was no longer working, and we needed to
find better ways to securely dissolve crowds. One recommendation from the Center for Policing Equity was

to make sure that everybody in the crowd heard our dispersal orders—we were told that not everybody heard our order to disperse because the crowd was so big. Even my own family complained they did not hear any orders or warnings because the police had begun using pepper spray and tear gas. We followed the suggestion and strategically placed a loudspeaker so that when we did give the order people could hear it and know what was happening.

Finally, we had to assess the damage. So many restaurants—whose income had plummeted compared to prepandemic standards—were severely damaged. Windows had been shattered and businesses looted. It was time to clean up and help the community. I was in awe as I saw private citizens rush to help business owners wipe off spray paint, restock shelves, and clean the floor of shattered glass. To me, this was a city in pain, afraid, and in desperate need of validation. And I shared their feelings. I, too, was stunned at just how deeply rooted systemic racism was in our country, so intrinsically sewn into the very fabric of the United States of America that many no longer even recognize its ugly face.

## Situational Leadership in Daily Life

We face situational leadership tests every single day in our personal lives, whether we realize it or not. An unexpected turn of events during a conference call, a child in need of sudden and immediate help, an episode of microaggression. I have often been on the receiving end of those ones. Microaggression, I mean. Let me give you the latest example. The other day, I had to update some documents, and the lady at the office desk read my address out loud and said, "Oh, I didn't know that Black people lived there too. Hmm, they must all be from the same family, I guess."

I looked at her and she looked at me, and suddenly I remembered what a dear friend of mine once told me: "I wake up in the morning and I go to wash my face. I look at myself in the mirror and I see a Black man. Then, I go out of the house, and I am reminded every step of the way that I am a Black man. The old lady who pulls her purse closer to her chest when I walk by her; the store clerk who keeps a close eye on me while I am at the store looking for my favorite drink; the bank teller who checks over and over that the money I wish to deposit is real and not fake. And I realize, I can't escape my Black face. Even when I'm not looking at myself in the mirror."

I thought about that story, and I knew all she saw was my Black face. I could tell that she had no idea about the racist nature of what she had just said. To her, there was absolutely nothing wrong with pointing out my race or the color of my skin and sharing that, to her, it was surprising that Black people could afford to live in that neighborhood. I also knew that I had just been faced with a situational leadership test—point out that microaggressions are intolerable and we are sick and tired of them, or grin and bear it because there's no point arguing with racist people? Some days you just have to choose your battles.

"Here are your documents."
I took them, smiled, and walked out of that office.
Another day, another microaggression.
Will they ever stop?

# TACTICAL DEBRIEF

**WHEN IT COMES** to leading an organization, a group of people, or an operation, it is not enough to have solid leadership skills. At one point or another, you will be faced with an unforeseen obstacle, an unpredicted confrontation, an unexpected emergency, and you must have the ability to think quickly on your feet and make the best possible decisions. But you must also remember that, whatever decision you make, it has ramifications. Your decision to place somebody in charge of a delicate matter might backfire and not produce the results you expected. Your decision to bring in help could put hundreds of lives at risk as opposed to saving them.

Being able to make a rational decision when faced with a situational leadership test is a skill that won't help you just in your professional life but in your personal life as well. And regardless of which route you choose, the decision-making process will never be easy. Because the one thing that all situational leadership matters have in common is that they are always uninvited.

1. Can you think of a time you faced a situational leadership test in the workplace?

2. Have you ever regretted the way you handled a situational leadership test? What would you do differently now?
3. How would you help your coworkers develop situational leadership skills?
4. When was the last time you faced a situational leadership test in your private life?

# 5

# Leadership Is a Lonely Place to Be

Leadership can be lonely. And that's a fact. When you are faced with some of the most challenging situational leadership tests of your career, you will often find yourself between a rock and a hard place. On one side, it's your profession: your colleagues, your department, and their expectations. On the other side, it's the media, with their politics, demands, and pressures. Both sides are loud. Both sides are strong willed. Both sides will complain, criticize, and ostracize you if you choose to do something they don't agree with. And somehow, you have to manage all that is coming at you from both fronts.

During the months of January through August 2020, while dealing with the mass shooting, the pandemic, the protests, and more, I often went back to my office and thought, *What is good?* and *What is bad?* and thought of my answers. I did so because I had to make sure that I upheld my obligation to act first and always as the Seattle Police Chief. I knew that, no matter what, I wasn't going to make everybody happy—that was just not a realistic outcome. It was in those moments, when I had to sit alone with my thoughts while the world was pressuring me, that I realized that leadership can indeed be lonely.

When you are charged with ensuring public safety in a jurisdiction, you have a commitment to enforcing the law and upholding the Constitution. You cannot make decisions based on what will "play well" in the media or what seems politically expedient or advantageous. But leading by doing what you know is right can leave you feeling alone.

In my career, I have learned the lesson that a crisis is not a time to ask someone to try something new. Even though it was tough, I had to make some team changes in the midst of everything that was going on. But the team came back together and again worked tirelessly for two straight months, after having just done that during COVID-19.

During the mass shooting, the outbreak of the pandemic, and the protests that followed George Floyd's murder, I knew that my team was working hard, and I knew that we had support from other law enforcement agencies. So when the opportunities presented themselves, I was happy to reciprocate and lend them a helping hand or an encouraging word. Yet it was during one of the toughest situational leadership tests of my entire career—harder than the previous ones that year—that all I found around me were doors slammed shut, phones quickly hung up, and a loud and clear "No!" I searched for help from other departments and organizations. I told them our department needed support, backup, help. Many people watched the situation in Seattle unfold—it seemed to me the whole world was— but no one else was standing up. These protesters were taking over part of a neighborhood, destroying property, attacking officers . . . all these things were just not right. But standing up was my job, and the only way I was going to keep the department engaged after taking weeks of rocks and bottles was to say: this isn't allowed! Of course, throughout it all, I made it clear I knew we would have to learn from our mistakes—I wasn't acting as if we did everything perfectly.

But I am getting ahead of the story here. So let me go back to the beginning . . .

## The Capitol Hill Autonomous Zone and Capitol Hill Occupied Protest

Demonstrations started right after George Floyd's death and carried through into June. The end of May and beginning of June proved to be intense weeks, with back-to-back demonstrations that had started downtown but eventually reached the East Precinct. During that time, several rioters committed a lot of property damage to businesses in Chinatown-International District until officers located them and were able to move them to another area. We had thousands of people demonstrating in downtown Seattle.

The officers and I closely monitored the demonstrations, making sure that people were safely exercising their constitutional rights. East Precinct commanders symbolically joined the demonstrators by kneeling down with them. Black Lives Matter members were there as well, reinforcing COVID-19 safety measures and reminding the crowd to stay at least five feet away from the barricades—so as not to threaten police officers. It all seemed to be under control.

Until it wasn't.

The situation had grown tense because elements of the crowd were becoming aggressive and attempting to breach the barricades one block from the East Precinct. Multiple times, police officers warned the crowds to move back, but the warnings did not accomplish anything. To the chant of "Take off your riot gear, we don't see no riot here!" members of the crowd showed no signs of de-escalation.

Many people opened umbrellas, a tactic reminiscent of the 2014 Umbrella Movement in Hong Kong when demonstrators—who were demanding the right to pick their own candidates as opposed to China's preapproved list of candidates—used umbrellas to defend themselves against tear gas used by police. One umbrella in particular stood out among the crowd: a rosy-magenta umbrella that would eventually become the symbol of the Seattle protests after one of the officers pulled it away from its holder. (The symbol was especially significant given that Seattleites do not normally use umbrellas to shield themselves from the rain.) The situation grew tense when some people within the crowd began throwing bottles, rocks, and fireworks at police officers, who responded with pepper spray and tear gas.

On June 8, we met with the mayor's office and city officials to discuss options for addressing the confrontations between some protesters and police standing the line. The mayor's staff advocated for taking barricades down, because they believed that, in doing so, people would calm down. My command staff did not want to move the barricades. We were very skeptical, but ultimately we decided to remove them and allowed the protesters to come in front of the building. The commanders were worried, however, that some in the crowd would burn down the building, as protesters had done in Minneapolis: we had a credible threat from the FBI that the East Precinct was a target. The fire chief said if they set the building on fire, it would burn down quickly. At that point, the commanders gave the order to police officers to vacate the precinct but not before gathering sensitive material and documents. This wasn't a permanent evacuation, but based on the recent burning down of a Minneapolis precinct, they wanted to be prepared in the event that things took a turn overnight and crucial police documents would have been permanently lost. They anticipated returning the next day after the crowds were gone, but that wasn't the case.

Instead, protesters replaced the police barricades with barricades of their own, and the Capitol Hill Autonomous Zone (CHAZ) started. At the beginning, the atmosphere there was nonviolent, with people giving speeches, distributing free food to those who joined, dancing, and watching movies. They renamed the streets Black Lives Matter Way and Black Lives Matter Square. "Entering Cop-Free Zone. Long live CHAZ," "This space is now property of the Seattle People," "Seattle People Department" were some of the spray-painted and written signs at the East Precinct.

Meanwhile, one city councilmember applauded the takeover and said the city should turn the precinct into a community center, but members of the Black Lives Matter movement were dedicated to preserving the wishes of the first African American city councilmember, Sam Smith, who had wanted the precinct to be in that very building. They came to my office telling me that someone in the mayor's office had offered them keys to the building, but the BLM leaders did not want to take it over. I could not believe what I had just heard.

To make matters worse, I knew the city council expressed its intent to review and cut the police department's budget, along with rethinking the way we ensured public safety. People also called for the mayor to resign. Personally, I was concerned that the protesters had taken over the East Precinct and that the police department's ability to respond to concerns in a timely fashion was thus hindered. I had signed up to help people, but being unable to operate from that building made that responsibility much more challenging. I wanted to reassure people that we could come together with the politicians, the activists, and the community and figure out how we could move forward by changing and evolving.

When I went to check on the situation at the building, somebody asked me why I was there. I simply answered: "Taxpayers are still paying for this facility. It's still costing them money and it's empty right now and it's disheveled and it's a mess. It's going to be a lot of work to make it functional again." Many of them shared their feelings regarding White privilege and the racism that permeates the criminal justice system.

"I am a Black woman," I said. "A chief trying to take care of public safety. My ancestors and your ancestors helped build community in slavery. And now here we are, trying to defend what's right and good. I'm going to quote Dr. Martin Luther King, because I love this quote: 'The time is always right to do what is right.' I will stand for what I believe is right. And people can agree or not agree because when I leave here, I'm still going to be the Black woman walking down the street, dealing with the issues that every other Black person is dealing with."

I wanted our community to know that we were there to help and support. When the officers first evacuated the East Precinct, even though I later discovered it was a false assumption, at the time, I thought, *The mayor must have given the order.* My head felt extremely warm; my breathing became labored. I couldn't think of another possible culprit. I knew that people in her office had been loudly expressing their disagreement with the way the police had handled the riots, and I assumed, incorrectly, she fell under the pressure. I was certain of it. I needed my officers to know the order to vacate did not come from me. I needed to tell my officers how I felt. So I recorded a video and released the following statement:

SPD Family,

I say that because that is what you are: you are my family. And family is honest with each other, and family has tough times but, in the end, we always remain family. We are all going through one of the toughest times ever in the history of the Seattle Police Department. I know how incredibly difficult these past two weeks have been for you and your families. To say "thank you" would never probably be enough but, thank you. This department cares about you. I care about you. And although it might not seem true in this moment, the community cares about you. I want to update you all about the situation at the East Precinct. The decision to board up the precinct, our precinct, our home, the first precinct I ever worked in, was something I have been holding off.

You should know, leaving the precinct was not my decision. We fought for days to protect it; I asked you to stand on that line day in and day out, to be hit with projectiles, to be screamed at, threatened, and in some cases hurt. Then to have a change of course nearly two weeks in . . . it seems like an insult to you and our community. Ultimately, the city had other plans for the building and relented to severe public pressure. I'm angry about how this all came about. I understand that my comments in this message may be leaked to the public, but I'm not concerned about that. I stand by what I'm saying. We had solid information to believe that anti-government groups would destroy the precinct once we left, whether through vandalism or arson.

As you might've heard, the Seattle Fire Department was nearby to protect the precinct and the entire residential block from a real risk of a large-scale fire. This week, there have been demonstrations and what I understand were threats against a news reporter on Capitol Hill. There was vandalism to our city streets and our building, but today, the precinct remains standing. No officers were hurt. No force was used. We have heard that there are armed people patrolling the streets near 12th and Pine. Of course, this is very concerning, especially because we don't know who these people are. We've also received report that these armed people may be demanding payment from business owners in exchange for some of that protection. We've also heard that they may be demanding to see identification from people who live in the area. This is not legal, and we've asked anyone who may be experiencing this to come forward and file a police report so that we can investigate these crimes.

In closing, I mostly just wanted to share how I feel. I am very thankful and very grateful for each and every one of you every single day. You are doing such incredible work, but I know you feel underappreciated. However, I do believe that most people in Seattle support the police department and its officers, even though they may not be the ones posting on social media. They and I will continue to have your backs, to support you and appreciate all that you are doing in the name of public safety.

Thank you and stay safe.[1]

Later on, once I learned that the mayor had not been the one to give the order, I apologized to her for assuming she had gone behind my back. My main concern, however, was not to find out who had done it but to reassure my officers and community that the order to give up the precinct had not come from me.

At the same time, I decided I wanted to reach out to the community to let them know that the police force was not only listening to their needs, but we were also being proactive in setting up a plan to begin to move forward:

The last few weeks in Seattle—beginning on May 25th, 2020, when George Floyd was murdered by a City of Minneapolis Police Officer—have been the most transformative and challenging moments, in my lifetime, for our City, and for the Seattle Police Department.

Just a few short months ago, before the full reality of a pandemic, and a social justice reckoning four-hundred years in the making, SPD submitted the last of the reports required under the federal consent decree. Across almost nine years of court-guided reform, SPD developed leading policies in crowd management, de-escalation, and use of force. These policies seem like ancient history now.

The federal consent decree achieved its goals—SPD has the training, supervision, analytics, and external oversights to ensure that the department continuously improves its response to demonstrations, people in crisis, use of force, and its overall transparency and sophistication. These efforts will ensure every event of the past few weeks is extensively reviewed, learned from, and when appropriate, responded to with full accountability.

Clearly, processes and policies are no longer enough to earn and maintain the trust of the community. What is now required is a complete re-envisioning of community safety and the police department's role in it. The only way this will be successful is if it is driven by community. To that end, SPD commits to doing this work with community. We have listened for generations, and we will continue to listen, but the time for talk and committees is over. We must act. Together.

Below, SPD outlines where it thinks these efforts can begin. These are barely first steps, but they are steps nonetheless. We welcome critical feedback and know this is the first of countless versions. You have my steadfast commitment, and word, that SPD will engage this work, openly and honestly. This will be on-going, but we also know there are immediate changes that must start today.

Sincerely,
Carmen Best

Chief of Police
Seattle Police Department

•  •  •

## RE-ENVISIONING COMMUNITY SAFETY IN SEATTLE

### INITIAL IDEAS AND CONSIDERATIONS

The Seattle Police Department knows that a new model of community safety will be completely different than any of the suggestions in this first outline. However, the experiences and perspectives of SPD officers and civilians should be included in whatever final version we all reach. SPD has embraced reform, and internal conversations confirm it is ready to push past the relative comfort of those efforts.

### REINVENT COMMUNITY ENGAGEMENT WITH SPD

SPD has worked with community for generations. We have supported advisory councils, liaison officers, Micro Community Policing Plans, Community Policing Teams, Safe Place, and much more. These have been traditional models of formally engaging the community. To truly re-envision community safety, community must do more than advise. They must lead. SPD proposes the following steps:

- Add a Community member to the SPD Command Staff
- Launch an on-going series of community collaboration sessions
- Conduct monthly Command Staff community meetings to receive feedback and respond in real time
- Create convenient online tools for direct community feedback on policy and operational changes

### REINVEST SPD RESOURCES IN COMMUNITY

SPD has voiced, for years, concerns that police officers are asked to play too many roles. Officers have become the safety net for a series of failures by other social systems—many of which are the result of sustained under-investment, as well as systemic racism. SPD is conducting a critical review of the work officers are called to engage in—by the community and by other government agencies. SPD needs to work with community to determine which of these responsibilities can acceptably be passed to other agencies, or completely turned over to the community.

- Assess non-criminal 911 calls, current outcomes, and alternate responses
- Determine an appropriate response to misdemeanor violations
- Reconsider the role of specialty units and proactive enforcement

## REDESIGN THE MISSION AND STRUCTURE OF SPD

SPD has focused on enforcing the law and maintaining the peace—its responsibility as outlined in the City Charter. SPD must craft, with community, an updated mission. This mission inherently will direct the structure of the department.

- Align the mission of the SPD to reflect humanization not criminalization
- Conduct a top-to-bottom redesign of the department to match the mission and goals
- Identify new metrics of success that reflect community safety, trust, and legitimacy[2]

I wanted people in the community to know that they had been heard. That I was not just a figurehead. I was a woman in uniform working for the betterment, safety, and longevity of our community. I had always put my service to the community at the top of my priority list, and I was certainly not going to change that now when people needed it the most. But time was running out, and we had to act quickly in regaining their trust so we could carry on with our service.

Things escalated quickly. Weeks had gone by since the occupation, and city agencies were handing out hand sanitizer and cookies to people of the CHOP! It was time to put a stop to this and clear it out.

It was standard procedure for us to call for backup and have other police departments and agencies send us some of their officers to help. So I began following protocol and called some of the police departments nearby. Nobody offered to help, except Bellevue Police Department. I suspected it was because the others were witnessing what was happening to the Seattle Police Department and wanted nothing to do with it. I called multiple agencies hoping they would send us help. Nobody came. It seemed we had become personae non gratae. All around, I was looking for help and support. My officers were the only ones willing to defend the precinct against elements of the crowd that had grown consistently more violent and aggressive. My officers, who had families at home waiting for them to come back safely, were the only ones standing up. We needed support.

And that's when I realized: leadership is lonely.

I resigned myself to the idea that we were not going to get help from anybody. I checked in with my commanders, who told me we needed just over three hundred officers to carry out the operation. I looked at them and said, "Well, we've got that many!" I knew it was a break from tradition. We had already used other agencies to help. This time we needed to use our own staffing to resolve the situation. So we came up with a game plan: we trained the officers to make sure that they knew how to extract people with little or no force, and taught them all the things they needed to do to have the least potential for bad optics or use of force. And then, to implement the operation, we had to evaluate what our legal authority was. Just because we're cops, that doesn't give us a special power to do as we please; we have to ensure we have the legal authority to operate. And that's why we always start operations and train our officers to ask, "What's our legal authority?"

We understood that we needed an executive order to remove people from their tents at CHOP. The day before the operation was scheduled to start, the city began drafting an executive order that would guide us in what we could and what we could not do and how we could execute the operation. This took an extremely long time, and I felt a reluctance for anyone to take responsibility, for the okay to fall on anyone's shoulders; instead, I felt they wanted the police department to bear the burden and face any fallout. I was furious. It was crazy.

Finally, sometime after 9:00 p.m. or so, the order was issued. We had roll call in the wee hours of the morning. I addressed the officers and told them, "Nobody is coming to help us. Look to your right and look to your left. This is all we have. It's just us. We have to take the East Precinct back, and we have to do it today. We are going in before five." I looked at them and added, "No matter what happens, if there's resistance, we need to rely on our training and use minimal force, but we need to keep going." This was a dangerous operation, and the officers knew it.

"Chief, you're going to get us killed!" said one of them.

"I promise you we will do our best to not have any injury to anyone, officers or others. But if you feel you are not up for it, then take off your uniform and go home." And that went for everybody.

None of the officers left. And I couldn't have been any prouder. Mission was a go. We knew this operation was going to last well throughout the whole day and possibly into the night. We prepared for it as much as we possibly could. The officers were well equipped and well trained—slow and methodical. It was approximately four in the morning on July 1, 2020. I held my breath the moment I knew the officers had initiated the operation. I was standing outside of a fire station a block away, listening to the updates on the radio. I kept pacing. Back and forth. Back and forth. And then, the news arrived. Within two hours, the East Precinct was once again under the control of the Seattle Police Department. Almost a month after the CHOP began.

While I wanted to take time to rejoice and celebrate the brave officers who had successfully carried out the mission, we knew we could not afford that luxury because *now* the real work began. There were still demonstrators and protesters who threatened to retake the building; the precinct was in shambles, and we needed to repair it and make it functional again; we had to deploy officers to protect not just the East Precinct but also the other buildings that the police department operated from. I wanted to serve my community. I wanted to lead the Seattle Police Department. Until I was faced with a choice that I never saw coming and that would force me to decide whether to give in to demands or stand by what I knew was right. But that is a story for the next chapter.

# TACTICAL DEBRIEF

**THERE COMES A** time when a leader must make a difficult decision and stand up for what's right. This is not easy to do, and most people will give into media pressure and public demand. Many will not offer help. Many will criticize you. Many will blame you. And you will have to lead alone. You will not have another choice, because your team will still look to you for leadership. You can't leave them alone; they depend on you. The community depends on you. The question is: Are you ready for it?

1. Did you ever find yourself having to lead alone?
2. Have you ever dealt with media pressure and public demands?
3. What would you say was the most challenging leadership situation you ever found yourself in?
4. Have you ever given in to public pressure and gone against your own values and beliefs? If so, what would you do differently if you had the chance?

# 6

# Leadership Won't Let You Sacrifice Your Values

"Thank you for what you have done for me personally and for this department. I'd finally been hired after applying for five years, and I was ecstatic that it was under your command. Being an African American male with you as my Chief made the fact that I had served my country under the honorable Barack Obama that much sweeter."

Officer Marcus Jones sent me this email on August 10, 2020, after I had announced my retirement from the Seattle Police Department. I remember meeting him: a tall, stout, and wonderful African American man doing temperature checks at the building entrance. And it just broke my heart that he was more than likely going to be one of the first people to lose his job because of the new budget cuts proposed by the city council in response to the whirlwind period we had just had. I cried when I read his email. My heart ached for him—he was so proud of his position and so hopeful for the future after seeing an African American man become the president of the United States of America and an African American woman become the first woman of color to cover the role of chief for the Seattle Police Department. Tears streamed down my cheeks as I thought of what my exit would mean for him, as well as the many other men and women who were about to lose their jobs—their livelihood—because of the city council's decision to cut 50 percent of our budget.

That night, I decided to print Marcus's email and place it in my white folder, which I was going to bring to the press conference the day after, where I planned to officially announce my retirement.

## Leadership and Values

Leadership is knowing that if you have to compromise your values to remain where you are, it's time to go. And that's exactly what I chose to do on August 11, 2020: I left. But before we get there, let me tell you how I reached this decision. It was certainly not one I took lightly. I hoped until the last minute that I did not have to leave the organization I had dedicated most of my adult life to. I cared about every single officer and employee, their needs, and their families. I cared about my community, from the pastors to the business owners. I cared about my daughters and what they thought of me, of the police, of the way the police treated the African American community and other minorities. That's why I fought so hard for what I believed in and cared for.

It all started when the police took back control of and reoccupied the East Precinct and protests slowed down. Loud calls to defund the police had been heard during the many weeks of demonstrations, and the demands had placed a lot of pressure on the city council, which decided to look into ways to cut the budget. At first, the proposed cut was 5 percent. I was more than happy to work alongside the city council and, together, come up with ways to save money. I offered a few solutions and opened the door for conversations between them and the police force.

But the situation turned for the worse when the council proposed a 50 percent cut or to even abolish the police force altogether in response to the Black Lives Matter demonstrations.

I felt aligned with what the Black Lives Matter movement stood for, and I agreed that we needed to do something to stop the high rate of police killings of Black people. But I didn't think defunding or abolishing the police was the solution. I just didn't see the answer to be a "one size fits all." Because the police force was not made up of only bad people. I knew that in our department the vast majority were good, hardworking, loyal, and faithful police officers who valued humanity. So, when the city council began tossing around ideas to abolish the police—to get rid of the department and start it over, without, from what I could tell, a plan by the way—or lay off 50 percent of the police department, my ears began to ring.

To abolish the police department was such an absurd concept that I couldn't even fathom it—again, I did not see a plan. So I focused on what defunding the police and cutting 50 percent of our officers meant. For us in Seattle, it meant that people who had been working at the department for eleven years or less were about to lose their jobs. We had just spent a substantial sum of money to bring on new officers and had put a lot of effort into a campaign called This Is My Neighborhood, aimed at recruiting local officers and increasing diversity. In 2019, we hired 108 people—the highest number of new hires in more than a decade—and 39 percent of them were non-White, which went a long way in diversifying our police force to better mirror the increasingly diverse population of the city. So the idea of having to lay off all these people was too much for me.

I spent weeks and weeks and weeks trying to get the council to listen to my worries, but they completely disregarded me. Why were they not willing to have an open line of communication with the police department? How can you think about reconstructing the department without understanding what the department does? I had been working at the Seattle Police Department for the past twenty-eight years, and I had served under Chief Kerlikowske, Chief Stamper, and Chief O'Toole. I served with almost every chief in some capacity, and I had never seen an instance where a police chief and command staff were just completely ignored. The council didn't want anything to do with me or with anything I had to say. They didn't want my opinion. They didn't want my thoughts. Nothing. I couldn't help thinking: *Are they dismissing me because I am a Black woman or is the city council refusing to include me because they don't want to be seen as working with the police?* Either way, it was clear that public safety was no longer their top concern.

All the city councilmembers were saying was, "We're going to defund." Yet I did not hear them asking, "Well, how might we do this?" I just found it unbelievable. Even if they were going to force officer layoffs, they should have had a plan on how to go about it. They should have talked to the people who understood the system. They just did not bother to engage me in the conversation— something that I perceived as extremely disrespectful. Why were they behaving this way? I also couldn't help thinking that they were upset over just how low they were in the public opinion polls—hovering around 25 percent approval. I couldn't imagine how I would feel at 25 percent. I wanted to improve the situation and do what was right by the community, but the city council was not interested in what I had to say. I kept reading about their decisions and ideas in the newspapers and on social media. These decisions and ideas were going to severely affect the police department that I was responsible for under the city charter. Yet they showed no interest in talking to *me*.

One idea they had was the possibility of replacing officers with social workers. I felt uneasy about the way they were going about it—with no plan. Who was going to train the social workers? How were they going to pay for them if they were cutting the budget? Was hiring social workers the only right answer to the overall concern of racism in police forces? Were they going under the assumption that there was no such thing as a racist social worker? Racism is a widespread systemic disease. It nestles within households and, at the first opportunity, escapes and spreads in school districts, neighborhoods, communities, and every single job and career.

Was the city council truly concerned with moving things forward and improving the quality of life for Seattle, or were they doing what they thought would make them popular? I believe that lack of public approval did play a role in what was happening. And it was particularly distressful, because the councilmembers were just vehemently rude. I had one telling me that, as women of color, we should be supporting each other. Yet she could muster little more than a verbal slap on the wrist for protesters continuing to destroy property and protesting at private residences. Another councilmember who consistently berated the department in the past for not doing enough about fireworks—fireworks!—was now calling for a 50 percent defunding of the department, including leading the call for targeted layoffs of officers to adjust for racial disparity. Another councilmember who was the same age as my daughter berated me and treated me in a manner that some considered racist when he cross-examined me during a council briefing as if I were on trial. I was so affected by his demeaning behavior that I wrote him a letter in which I highlighted the many microaggressions he had thrown at me.

The atmosphere between me and the city council was contentious because they would not listen or take anything that I had to say into account. Two councilmembers attempted to get their colleagues to slow down and think. But, like me, they were shut out. It was another sign that the die had been cast, and despite the facts on the ground, any sense of thoughtful engagement and deliberation was just a show.

They were not willing to have a dialogue about reimagining or re-envisioning policing. There was no such thing as "How do we make things better? Let's have a discussion about it. Let's go to the table with all of the stakeholders." Nothing. It felt as though it was a very organized, systematic way of shutting us out. And I was not going to stand for it. I had to find a way to communicate and get on the record. I knew they were not going to invite me to talk to them, so I reached out to them in the only way they would understand: via the press. I wrote a lengthy and detailed response to their proposed budget cuts and other outlandish ideas and published it on the Seattle Police Department Blotter. I knew that, even if they were not going to read it, the press would talk about it and, as such, they would be forced to hear my voice through the media.

Dear President González, Chairwoman Herbold,
and Seattle City Councilmembers:

In the spirit of working collaboratively toward a new vision of community safety in this city, I wanted to take this opportunity to provide the police department's perspective on the proposals currently in front of council. Seven City Councilmembers committed to cutting 50% of the SPD budget—some of you have later clarified that this is 50% of SPD's budget from August 2020–December 2020, which would require SPD to cut $85 million and require a simply irresponsible number of layoffs. I understand Councilmember Sawant has detailed her reductions, which would require reductions of 681 of 755 members of patrol.

As you and the other Councilmembers are quickly considering significant budget actions, I cannot stress strongly enough how critical it is that you include SPD in the discussions in order to understand the foreseeable impacts and repercussions of any proposed cuts from Council or the Decriminalize Seattle/King County Equity Now proposals. As you are becoming more aware, any action in 2020 will potentially have significant implementation, labor, legal, or public safety implications.

I have stated, clearly and repeatedly, that SPD stands ready to engage in a community-led re-envisioning of community safety. SPD has a robust history of seeking community guidance—formally and informally—and will never shy away from authentic engagement with its varied and diverse communities. I also fully understand, and support, significant investment of funds into community-based safety resources—investments that SPD has long been on record as supporting. I am gravely concerned, however, that by creating a false dichotomy between funding police services and investing in the community—where investments in services upstream of police intervention necessarily come at the expense of depleting police resources—Council is omitting from its analysis the decades of experience that so many in SPD have. This department has demonstrated, time and again in the past almost ten years, its ability to change how it operates, to be more transparent, to engage the nation's experts, and to listen to community.

It also is important to acknowledge that many of these recommendations intersect directly with the requirements and work of the federal Consent Decree—reforms that were, as the Consent Decree itself notes, guided by substantial community involvement. It is concerning to me that so many who just weeks ago urged the federal court to stay involved now question the reforms that were enacted, but the court still retains jurisdiction and neither through legislation nor budget action can we cease to abide by the commitments we all have made. While this letter will be followed by a more detailed analysis of SPD training, policies, and practices that were guided by the Consent Decree, I do want to make sure I am on record, now, as at least flagging these issues for preliminary awareness.

Lack of awareness of these issues is not an indication of a need for more transparency; rather, it is a clear indication of not doing the work that should be done before making these sorts of wide-ranging recommendations. The federal settlement agreement is available online for all to read. The SPD policy manual is available online for all to read. SPD data are available online—in dashboard and raw form—for all to review and use.

Apart from the specific recommendations, I also must point out that as a department we believe in science. There is a plethora of evidence that effective, evidence-based policing prevents crime. I do not know what the advocates were pointing to when they stated to council, they have evidence that policing doesn't prevent crime, but there are countless, peer-reviewed articles that confirm the exact opposite.

Altogether, I am concerned by the clear disconnect many of these recommendations have from reality. If we are to do the hard work ahead of us, we cannot argue about facts. If we are going to successfully meet the needs of our entire community, we must, together, create a plan, grounded in theory, guided by evidence, and governed by equity. With a plan in place, we can then, as a City, determine how to best fund and implement that plan. This will not happen overnight. We will have to "bridge the gap" between the realities of today and the vision of tomorrow. I hope the guidance provided below, in response to each recommendation, is part of the conversation.

## DECRIMINALIZE SEATTLE/KING COUNTY EQUITY NOW RECOMMENDATIONS & SPD RESPONSES

- Freeze hiring. Any planned hiring, including for individuals in the training pipeline, should be cancelled.
- Earlier this year, SPD met its hiring goals for 2020. The Mayor and SPD have frozen additional hiring through 2021 until further workforce and staffing analysis can be completed.
- City Councilmembers overwhelmingly supported SPD's new hiring and recruitments that have led to historic diversity in the department. However, SPD has serious concerns about removing recruits and individuals who are currently training with SPD as it could impact public safety. It should be noted, that of those 51 individuals "in the pipeline" and hired in 2020 before the hiring freeze was initiated, 37% are individuals of color.

- ○ **Consent Decree**—The City is required to provide SPD with adequate numbers of qualified field/first-line supervisors. Significant cuts, direct or through attrition, will jeopardize the department's ability to meet this requirement.
- ○ The de-escalation and use of force principles developed during the Consent Decree are heavily based on evidence that reducing solo-officer dispatches reduces use of force incidents. Stretching SPD staffing resources would completely go against this research and potentially lead to increases in uses of force. SPD has shown, in the federal monitor's cited 60% reduction of serious uses of force, that these principles work. SPD uses any level of force in less than one quarter of 1 percent of all events, with the vast majority of that force categorized as the lowest level, Type I.

- Eliminate funds for recruitment and retention, including bonuses for new hires.
- ○ **Consent Decree**—As noted above, SPD must have adequate staffing to ensure sufficient and consistent supervision. Significant reductions in staffing through direct action or attrition will jeopardize compliance.
- ○ The Executive and SPD have ended all recruitment and retention expenditures and allowed the hiring bonus program to lapse in June 2020, as hiring bonuses were no longer necessary to attract the best applicants. While the initiative was stopped, the funding currently supports 2.75 FTE that have

been redirected to the City's response on COVID-19 and other projects.

○ Considering the City has a longstanding commitment to fair wages, the department intends to honor the contracts entered into under the hiring incentive program—it would be unconscionable to break these contracts. As previously noted, City Council overwhelmingly supported creating and expanding hiring bonuses.

• Remove the Office of Collaborative Policing, including Navigation Team. While some programs of this office, along with administrative infrastructure, should be eliminated altogether, others could be moved to a civilian-controlled agency. Eliminate: Navigation Team, Community Outreach Administration

○ After community input, I created the Collaborative Policing Bureau, which is led by Chief Adrian Diaz. We reorganized the Department to form a Collaborative Policing Bureau and focus our civilian and sworn officers on education, mentorship, and, perhaps most importantly, youth safety and intervention. The Bureau includes CSOs, civilian contracted Mental Health Professionals, and the sworn Crisis Intervention Team.

○ In 2020, SPD expanded, and Council approved, the number of contract, civilian, MHPs who advise and respond to crisis incidents throughout the City. SPD advises against cutting the civilian mental health professionals.

- ○ Many of the community's favorite outreach programs—Detective Cookie's Chess Club, The IF Project, Seattle Police Athletics League, Safe Place—would no longer be possible with the elimination of this unit, coupled with staffing reductions and the elimination of overtime.
- ○ Fiscal Impact from Aug–Dec 2020: Cutting the entire bureau would lead to approximately a reduction of 1.3% of SPD's budget. Understanding a blunt cut to the bureau doesn't account for expenses that can't be reduced mid-year or instantly including benefits, equipment, and supplies.
- ○ **Consent Decree**—the settlement agreement specifically requires a partnership between the SPD, its officers, community members, and public officials.
- ○ The Navigation Team is based in the Human Services Department. The SPD officers and sergeants assigned to the City's Navigation Team are supervised in the Collaborative Policing Bureau.

- • Transfer out of SPD control: Crisis Intervention Response, Community Service Officers
- ○ In addition to King County's 24/7 Crisis Line, SPD currently responds to over 10,000 crisis calls a year. The Crisis Intervention Team are sworn officers that can't be transferred.
- ○ **Consent Decree**—The settlement agreement specifically requires that SPD maintain sufficient, trained officers on all shifts to respond to incidents or calls involving individuals known or suspected to

have a mental illness, substance abuse, or behavioral crisis need.

○ Under the Revised Code of Washington, only sworn peace officers can initiate an Involuntary Treatment order in the field.

○ Sworn crisis officers are necessary to support the Extreme Risk Protection Order program. To date, this unit has seized over 150 guns from individuals at risk of hurting themselves or others.

○ Chief Best and Mayor Durkan, with Council approval, have relaunched the Community Service Officer program

- Eliminate spending on new equipment
○ While it could lead to relatively minor savings, there are multiple instances where occupational safety requirements, legal considerations, and other personnel requirements mandate the provision of sufficient equipment in good, working order.

○ Defective or out-of-date equipment places officers and others at risk.

- Eliminate Data-Driven Policing
○ **Consent Decree**—The on-going analysis of data on officer actions, with accompanying public reports, by SPD, is directly required by the settlement agreement.

○ It is unclear what this means, but if the suggestion is to cease employing civilian analysts who both respond to countless requests for data and analyses, as well as ensure the department is measuring what it is doing—and its impacts, this would go against all best practices in policing and in modern organizational management. This team has been the driving force behind sharing data in public dashboards, datasets, and outside researcher engagement.

- Eliminate spending on North Precinct Capital Project
- The Executive and SPD have canceled this work.


- Eliminate Professional Services—Photo Enforcement, Sworn Hiring in HR, Recruitment and Retention, Community Outreach, Implicit Bias Training, Communications
- **Consent Decree**—Implicit Bias Training is specifically required under the settlement agreement.
- Sworn Hiring in HR—The SPD must conduct the background investigation of all individuals conditionally offered employment as outlined in the RCW.
- Photo Enforcement—This funding pays for the City's vendor contract for the Red Light Camera Enforcement Program. Elimination of this program would have revenue impacts.
- Recruitment and Retention—SPD will need to ensure, as outlined above under staffing requirements, sufficient staffing, and cannot fully eliminate this function moving forward.
- Community Outreach—the issues with eliminating the funding and overtime for this work are previously outlined in the discussion of the Collaborative Policing Bureau.

○ Communications—This funding supports the contract for translation services for calls received by the 911 Communications Center.

- Cut SPD's spending on Homeland Security (a misnamed unit that is mostly assigned to large events like Bumbershoot and sporting events)
○ It should be clearly stated that SPD's Homeland Security Bureau in no way relates to the federal agency of the same name. It should have its role clarified with a more appropriate title. This unit coordinates security at all major events in the city, and cutting it would lead to issues staffing these events. The City's general fund is reimbursed $5.7M a year in these event costs as revenue. Any major event that requires overriding traffic signals must be done by sworn officers in accordance with RCW.

- Eliminate SWAT Team funding
○ The City of Seattle is designated as an Urban Areas Security Initiative (UASI) Level 2 city and has the recommended SWAT staffing for this designation.
○ The SWAT Team primarily responds to barricaded subjects, active shooter incidents, dignitary protection, hostage rescue, and high-risk warrant services. Eliminating this unit would not eliminate the need for it and would result in lesser-trained and equipped officers having to respond to these events, increasing the risk to everyone involved. Only sworn law enforcement officers can serve warrants. Of note, SWAT is modeled after best

practices that were developed in part upon recommendations promulgated following the stabbing death of a King County Deputy and subsequent stand-off in the 1980s.

- End contracts with private firms that defend SPD and the City against police misconduct lawsuits
- This would not result in SPD budget savings. Just as outside counsel is often appointed for other city employees, including Council at large or councilmembers individually, all outside counsel use for any City business are paid for through the Judgement Claims Fund. Outside counsel are obtained when the City Attorney's Office lacks capacity or a specific expertise. With the exception of punitive damages, which, to SPD's knowledge, have never been part of a judgment against the City relating to a police action case, the City is required to defend and indemnify all employees for acts or omissions within the scope of their duties.

- Eliminate SPD's travel and training budget
- The Mayor and SPD included a $596,000 cut to SPD's travel and training budget in the 2020 rebalancing proposal. This funding left is expected to be used for travel and required training and certifications.
- **Consent Decree**—The settlement agreement specifically outlines requirements for annual training for all officers across many areas. This would be in direct conflict.

○ SPD is responsible, as an employer, to ensure its workforce is appropriately trained to do the job they are required to do. Not doing so would significantly open the City up to lawsuits both from employees and any individuals who suffered any injury due to inadequate training.

○ Executive Leadership Training: Good governance recognizes the importance of continuing education in executive leadership, staying abreast of best practices, and learning from other organizations and academic partners who have dedicated their careers to advancing the social science of policing. Across the board, SPD's command staff—half of which comprises civilians with advanced degrees of JDs, Ph.D.s, and Masters of Public Administration, and half of which comprises sworn personnel with decades of experience, engagement, and continuing education—has dedicated itself, and in many instances, their own time and money, to engaging at the national level to bringing SPD to the leading edge of police reform.

• End overtime pay, including for Emphasis Patrols
○ The Mayor and SPD have already proposed reductions to SPD's overtime in 2020 in the amount of $8.6M. As of July 7, 2020, SPD expended $21,921,109 on overtime, or 104 percent of its total overtime budget. There is no budget remaining.

○ Overtime pay is a bargained right of many employees. There are countless scenarios—be it completing required investigative paperwork or responding to a large-scale emergency—where it is not possible to avoid overtime hours and they must be compensated.

○ Overtime is frequently used to ensure adequate staffing when unexpected absences lead to unsafe staffing levels. Overtime also is the only method at current staffing levels to ensure there are sufficient instructors to provide state and court-mandated training.

- Reduce patrol staffing, with corresponding reduction in administrative staffing

○ Emergency response services are the core of the City's police powers and its chartered responsibility to establish social order, protect life and health of persons, and to safeguard individuals in their enjoyment of private and social life and use of their property. As I previously have noted, if Council wants to cut patrol, it will lead to significant layoffs, closure of precincts, including the Southwest Precinct, and slower response times.

- Transfer 911 dispatch out of Seattle Police Department to civilian control

○ The Executive and Chief of Police have proposed this move. The personnel in the Communications center who receive and dispatch emergency calls are all civilian employees, as are frontline supervisors. Police officers do not receive or dispatch calls for service. This proposal will likely

need to be bargained and cannot be fully
implemented until late 2020/early 2021.

- Transfer traffic/parking enforcement out of SPD control
  - The Executive and Chief of Police have proposed
    the move of PEOs. Per the union, this proposal will
    need to be bargained and cannot be fully
    implemented until bargained.

- Transfer Office of Police Accountability out of SPD
  control
  - The Executive and Chief of Police have proposed
    this move for 2021, and the Mayor and Chief have
    committed to continued conversations with OPA to
    ensure any labor issues are addressed.

- Reduce administrative costs in line with the above
  cuts, including corresponding cuts to the office of the
  Chief of Police, Leadership and Administration, and
  Administrative Operations.
  - **Consent Decree**—the settlement agreement speaks
    specifically to the requirements on administrative
    positions to oversee the use and review of uses of
    force. This is in direct conflict with the
    requirements.
  - Many administrative positions support local, state,
    and federal reporting requirements.
  - It is well-established that the Chief of Police is
    responsible for the administration of the Police
    Department and is the City's official policymaker for
    law enforcement.

As I have said countless times during the current turmoil, the Seattle Police Department stands ready to engage the important conversations and work to produce real, lasting change in community safety. That change, however, must be met with a plan. While again, I will follow this letter with one that lays out specific legal and practical issues we see, I hope these details clarify the risks inherent in undermining the Consent Decree, best practices, and labor agreements, without thought-out proposals informed by experience and research.[1]

Sincerely,
Carmen Best
Chief of Police

Yet even after my umpteenth attempt to connect with them, all I heard back was silence. And silence hurt even more than words. At one point, one of the people in the city council suggested that I could pick and choose whom I would have to fire. And that proposal left me even more baffled. What was I supposed to do? Lay off all my White officers? I could not believe she would make such a suggestion. I shook my head and became even more disheartened by how the council was behaving.

Meanwhile, public unrest grew louder, and protesters took over again. This time, however, they did not target the precinct. Rather, they came straight into my neighborhood. Once again, I asked for the city council's support and help via the SPD Blotter, the only way I felt would allow my voice to be heard by them.

Dear President González, Chairwoman Herbold,
and Seattle City Council Members:

I wanted to update you on recent events, particularly those that
occurred late last night. A residence of mine in Snohomish
County was targeted by a large group of aggressive protestors
late last night. My neighbors were concerned by such a large
group, but they were successful in ensuring the crowd was not
able to trespass or engage in other illegal behavior in the area,
despite repeated attempts to do so. Currently, the local sheriff
(not SPD resources) is monitoring the situation. I urge both of
you, and the entire council, to stand up for what is right. These
direct actions against elected officials, and especially civil servants like myself, are out of line with and go against every dem-
ocratic principle that guides our nation. Before this devolves
into the new way of doing business by mob rule here in Seattle,
and across the nation, elected officials like you must forcefully
call for the end of these tactics. The events of this summer were
initiated in a moment of grief and outrage over the murder of
George Floyd by Minneapolis police officers and so many other
Black and Brown people suffering at the hands of injustice. All
of us must ensure that this righteous cause is not lost in the
confusion of so many protestors now engaging in violence and
intimidation, which many are not speaking against.[2]

Sincerely,
Carmen Best

Result? Nothing. And that was when I reached the
point of no return. I could see the writing on the wall:
the city council was going to let me be the scapegoat for

mass layoffs. While it would be their budget decision, you can be certain the media headlines and labor grievances would be centered on me. They would say they couldn't tell the chief what to do and that they can only decide the budget. And I was not going to let them dictate my legacy. That was not a legacy I was willing to buy into, especially after people worked so hard to improve the department and bring on these wonderful new public servants.

I had no choice but to stand by my values and beliefs. I believed that the police profession needed to change and improve. I believed that we needed to work together with the council to come up with a solid plan on how to move forward. I believed that we needed to listen to our community and its needs. I did not believe that mass layoffs were going to solve anything. I did not believe that silence between the authorities was going to solve anything. I did not believe that silence between leaders was going to solve anything. I did not believe that replacing 50 percent of police officers with social workers was going to wipe out racism. I cared about my officers, every single one of them. From the most senior to our most recent recruit. I cared about their families. I cared about my community and what it meant to the people there if, suddenly, there were 50 percent fewer officers out there to protect them, their businesses, their lives. I cared. And it was because I cared that I chose to step down.

So, on August 11, 2020, I walked into my office and took a good look at all the photos I proudly displayed on the shelves around the room. Those were photos of my family, who always inspired me to keep going. As my eyes traveled along the shelves, they ran across many coins I had received in my career as a symbol of appreciation and partnership from other law enforcement partners. I looked up at a higher shelf and saw books and more books that focused on the city as well as the role I had covered over the past three decades in protecting it. As I sat down in my chair, I couldn't help thinking of the pivotal lessons I had learned throughout the years: from my parents, who taught me to work hard, because there is no success without hard work; from my peers, who taught me the importance of building genuine relationships and to stand up for what I believe is right; from my mentors, allies, and sponsors, who taught me that leadership is full of unpredictable challenges but that they will always be there to support me and show me the way, even when it gets lonely.

"Chief, we're ready," one of the officers told me, startling me from my train of thought. I looked up and smiled, letting him know I was ready as well. He walked behind the camera—positioned six feet away from me, thus following COVID-19 safety measures—ready to start recording the message I was about to deliver. I took a deep breath, glanced at a photo of my daughters, and looked straight into the camera as I spoke to my officers, my community, and my family: "Two years ago, I stood before my family and friends and raised my right hand and was sworn in as the chief of your police department. And today, I want to let you all know that I will be retiring, effective September 2. I promised to protect this community and this wonderful city. I had been a police officer for almost thirty years, and becoming the chief of police was the dream of a lifetime. I love this community, I love the city, and I love the Seattle Police Department. But over the years, I have learned that you will know when it's time to go. And for me, it's time. This decision was not easy for me. From Chinatown-International District to Rainer Beach, from Ballard to Madison Park, from downtown to West Seattle, and every neighborhood in between, they all mean the world to me.

"To my friends, the community, thank you. I grew up here and have big goals and big dreams. Hard work and support from this community got me to where I am today. And I am eternally grateful to you. This department, its people mean everything to me. I worked in patrol addressing quality of life issues. I worked in gang and robbery units addressing violent crime. I worked in the schools and community outreach, where I partnered with the clergy, neighborhood leaders, and immigrant families to make a difference in our most underserved communities. Police work is the greatest profession in the world. This department is full of the very best public safety professionals out there. And I've been honored to work alongside the men and women of the Seattle Police Department. You inspire me. You've kept me focused in the good times and the bad, and I could not have done it without your support. Thank you.

"Even though I'm retiring, I will always consider myself a member of this incredible department. I have no regrets. I feel so blessed and fortunate to have had this job and to call you all my brothers and sisters. I want to thank Mayor Jenny Durkan for her support. The mayor has named my deputy chief, Adrian Diaz, as the interim chief. Deputy Chief Diaz has spent his entire career committed to serving the city of Seattle. He has deep roots in this community, and he cares so much about our neighborhoods and our youth. He will work tirelessly as an advocate for equity and justice. He is ready for this challenge. I ask that you continue to support each other and to support him. I am grateful for the bonds and friendships that I've developed over the years in this community and with all of you. And I will carry those with me. It has truly, truly been an honor to serve as your chief. Thank you."[3]

The camera light turned off.

I stood up, looked back at my shelves, and smiled.

It was time to go.

# TACTICAL DEBRIEF

**BEING THE LEADER** means that you must be aware of when it's time to pass the baton. While each one of us will make this pivotal decision on our own time, I chose to make mine when I was faced with a reality I simply could not condone. I knew what I valued and what I believed in. I knew what I stood for. I knew what I was not going to do. And that's when I decided it was time to go. Of course, I did not come to the decision lightly. It was a tough process that I tried hard not to go through. I did all I could think of to foster an open line of communication with those in charge. But my many attempts were met with silence and avoidance. I was not going to be a pawn in their schemes. I was not going to be the one to fire Officer Marcus Jones or any other of the latest recruits that the Seattle Police Department went to great lengths to secure in order to diversify the police force. I was not going to let that be my legacy. I had to take my story into my own hands and dictate what I wanted my legacy to be.

1.  Have you ever found yourself in a similar situation when you felt that the only way to stay at the organization you

worked for was to compromise your values, your beliefs, and yourself?

2. If you were to be faced with such a challenge, would you stay or would you resign?

3. What does your legacy mean to you?

# 7

# Leadership Does Not End at Retirement

After I announced my retirement, the same people—allies, mentors, and sponsors—who had stood by me throughout my career and who had let their voices be heard when I was suddenly dropped as a candidate from the position of chief rallied in the streets again to the sound of "Chief Best is the best!" I was deeply moved by how loudly they spoke up against racism and sexism—which they believed was the real reason the city council had pushed so hard to make me the scapegoat of mass layoffs and budget cuts. And they touched me with their belief in my leadership skills and their commitment to publicly and privately showing me their support. I received countless emails from allies who were anxious about the status of policing and feared it would only get worse after my retirement; pastors camped on the streets and prayed for my well-being and the well-being of the country after my retirement; my colleagues and the mayor stood by me in a relentless show of support.

All of them warmed my heart and proved to me that my hard work had been recognized and that I had made an impact on their lives, the community, and the city we all loved and cared about so much. They motivated me to keep going, to keep being the leader they needed me to be: the proud Black voice that spoke of the thin blue line.

## Leading from the Sidelines

Leadership does not end when you retire. And that is because leadership is a skill set that cannot be applied just in the workplace. That is why, even after I retired in September 2020, I still continue to be involved in policing, although not in the same capacity that I had served in the past three decades. I am currently a law enforcement analyst for KING 5, a law enforcement commentator for MSNBC, and chair of the Human Civil Rights Committee for the International Association of Chiefs of Police. I help with the Law Enforcement Immigration Task Force, work for a private security company, and help with many other committees, charities, and organizations. My heart will always be in policing and, of course, in helping the Black and Brown community—as well as other minority groups—so that we no longer have to witness the heartbreaking sight of a mother mourning over the loss of her child killed by the hands of a racist police officer. I spent a long time thinking of possible solutions to our many issues within the police force. And below are a few of the many ideas I have on how to reform policing without defunding or abolishing it.

**Establishing a Level of Discernment:** By now, you have learned that I am a huge supporter of the Black Lives Matter movement and a firm believer in not abolishing the police or defunding it to the point that police officers can no longer keep their job or carry out their daily tasks—as was the case when the city council in Seattle decided we had to do with 50 percent less money. There are other solutions that can be considered that are not as drastic—or dangerous, might I add—as defunding or abolishing the police. For example, I believe that people should not be penalized because of their economic circumstances. Let me give you an example: if a person who makes ten dollars an hour and has three children, rent or mortgage payments, and other bills is pulled over and cited for a noncriminal act, they should not have their license suspended because of it. Why? Because working-class people cannot afford to pay the ticket or court fees—which increase with time. Don't get me wrong; I am not suggesting that people who break the law should not be held accountable. On the contrary, they absolutely must be. I don't agree with what some of our councilmembers want to do and simply give a "get out of jail free card" to poor people. No, there needs to be some sort of bona fide proof that their circumstances really put them in a place where they can't afford to pay now for a noncriminal traffic violation. However, as I have also said before, I am not a believer of "one size fits all." We should look into each person's background and financial situation before charging them with an exorbitant amount of money they simply cannot afford to pay. What if, instead of charging them even more if they fail to show up in court, we give them a onetime pass because, at the end of the day, we are all human beings, and you or I, too, could forget that we have to be somewhere at a certain time. Let's establish a level of discernment and, perhaps, instead of charging a single mother who makes minimum wage the entire lump sum of the ticket and court fees, we could put them on a payment plan for six months and have them make minimum payments of, say, five dollars a month. This could be a better alternative than stacking on punitive fees and penalizing even more those who committed noncriminal violations and are already struggling financially to support their family. In a nutshell, before demanding to defund or abolish the police force—without having a solid plan to carry it out, by the way—we need to revisit and reform bail and ticketing by using a more compassionate, humanitarian, and equal lens.

**Focus on the Militia as a Whole:** We should never focus on the single member of a militia group but on the militia group as whole. Take the case of Timothy McVeigh, for example. He was the domestic terrorist responsible for the Oklahoma City bombing of 1995 that killed 168 people and injured 680 more—the deadliest act of terrorism before September 11, 2001, in the United States. He was executed by lethal injection on June 11, 2001. Did his death solve the problem? Apparently, no. What many failed to investigate was if the domestic terrorist had associations with any militia or terrorist groups. Twenty years later, a Michigan militia group accused of planning to kidnap Michigan governor Gretchen Whitmer was found to have had ties to Timothy McVeigh himself. This means that, when the domestic terrorist was taken into custody, all the other people involved in the militia group he was affiliated with were let free to go and hide underground and plan many other criminal acts. By cutting off the head of one snake, they allowed countless more to grow from it.

**Rely More on Local Law Enforcement:** To fight and prevent crime, it is pivotal that we begin to rely more on local law enforcement rather than having to rely so much on the Federal Bureau of Investigation—which has about four thousand people, while local law enforcement has thousands of people all over. Local law enforcement agencies know when something is amiss because they know the neighborhood and can often help discover when there are people out to harm others. I do believe that if the federal government were to work much more closely with local authorities, we could increase crime prevention. As I tried time and time again to let the Seattle City Council know, collaboration among authorities is pivotal in solving difficult situations. Don't you think that if a neighbor or a friend of yours or a family member has the intention of committing an illegal act—depending on the nature of the crime, of course—you might know sooner than the FBI?

**Hire More Women:** While I was chief, I made it a point to hire more women and people from minority groups because I believe that representation is important in every profession, including the police force. As I have already mentioned, however, across the country, law enforcement female hires do not even make up 15 percent! The data baffles me because we, as women, have worked so hard and fought so much to finally achieve equality. Yet we are still underpaid and not represented in what is essentially public service. Why? I believe the reason lies in the way police officers are portrayed and the narrative surrounding them by the media. We often associate the term *police* with racist White men. While there are, unfortunately, some racist White men in policing, it is not right to generalize because I, personally, have had the chance to work with exceptional White men and women, as well as people of color, while in policing. And that is exactly the reason why I am a big supporter of enhancing the number of women in the police force. Let's face it: most of what this job is, is connecting with people on a very personal level about whatever is going on with them in their lives. Who better than a woman could empathize with another woman who has been hurt either emotionally or physically? Who better than a woman could empathize with a woman whose child's safety has been jeopardized? Women are born leaders. Women are born compassionate. These two qualities make for a great police officer.

**Multiple Background Checks to Spot the Criminals:** As I have written before, not all cops are racists and not all racists are cops. Racism is a seed planted within the household that is nurtured by family members and peers and that soon spreads outside of the house and into the neighborhood, community, and country. It is our job as leaders of a group, organization, or company to recognize racism and fire it. We cannot, under any circumstance, put our head in the sand and think we would never hire a racist. But here is what I want you to keep in mind: the person you just hired might not be part of a separatist group now, but that does not mean they will not be part of one in the next year or two or ten. Do you normally do background checks on people who have been working for you for the past ten years? I don't think so. But I believe it is time to review this policy as well and start carrying out regular background checks, even on our most senior employees, to make sure their values still align with the organization they work for. Do you think that employees would engage in racist, criminal, and dangerous behavior if they knew that their employer was going to run a background check on them at any given time? Take the people who stormed Capitol Hill in Washington, DC, on January 6, 2021, for example. Do you think that a background check would have stopped them from showing up—or at least made them think twice before going? Personally, I believe so. And I'll be honest with you: I have fired a few of my officers for inappropriate behavior that, to me, was sexist and/or racist, and that clearly was not in the best interests of Seattle's public safety. Two of them in particular come to mind. While I was chief, it was brought to my attention that one of the officers wrote on his personal social media account something to the effect of "Gawd, I'm not inciting violence, but Hillary Clinton and President Obama need to stop lying." He embellished the post with the picture of a bomb, which I did not appreciate, especially because of the then recent bombings in Austin, Texas—which occurred in March 2018. I remember that, after he went through the entire disciplinary process—which begins with a chief, then it moves on to the Office of Professional Accountability, fellow police officers, and then civilians—the result recommended days off. I recall that after I read the suggested punishment for that behavior, I began fuming. I could not believe that he had blatantly made such a public statement and was going to walk free with just a few days off work. I wanted him to be punished, and clearly, I needed to go about it in a different way. So I reached out to the Secret Service and told them this officer had made threats against the former secretary of state and the former president. They listened to me and opened an investigation to how viable those threats were. After confirming the facts, they put his name on a list and, eventually, decided to terminate his employment. Another time, it was brought again to my attention that an officer I had known for a little more than twenty years had sent his former girlfriend racist remarks while he was off duty. I guess what happened was the couple then broke up because he did something to hurt her, and she decided to make these text messages known. One of the messages read that he did not want to work for a Black lesbian because he didn't like female cops. I confronted him, and he defended himself by saying that those were private messages he had sent on his own free time while off police property, so I should have just ignored those statements. To which I responded: "That's just like saying that you get to wear a KKK hood on your own time and we have to ignore it because you did not do it on police property. It doesn't matter!"

## What's Next in Leadership?

I am often asked: It seems like every day there is a new story of a White police officer killing an African American man or woman . . . is this ever going to end? This is a good question to ask and a difficult one to answer. I don't think "end" is the right verb to use because it is so definite. But I am truly hopeful for the future. We need to revisit, reimagine, or re-envision how policing is going to look in America. We have to hold people accountable for their actions. We need to punish those who were in violation of the law. We need radical change. But I know we can make great strides.

Actually, I believe we *have made* great strides. I was born in the 1960s, and in many ways, my childhood was much better than the one my mother experienced. And my daughter's childhood was much better than mine. We now have Black journalists to sit beside White journalists and talk about race from their point of view, adding to the conversation and making sure the public gets to hear and learn about different experiences. We have Black politicians who are able to debate with White politicians and point out what is wrong with certain laws and situations. We have diversity in the newsroom, in law enforcement, and in the White House. We finally have the proverbial seat at the table.

But we still have ways to go because we are still fighting to make our voices be heard just as loudly and well as our White peers; we are still struggling to keep our African American sons and daughters alive during regular traffic stops; we are still trying to improve the life conditions and expectancy of the American people who recognize themselves as being members of a minority group. We still have a lot of work ahead of us. And in order to work hard to better ourselves and our nation, we have to work together to come up with a plan we are proud of and can safely put into action.

There must be an open line of communication among the many organizations and authorities. Silence must be abolished because silence feeds racism and sexism. Silence is a bigoted society. So, if we wish to fix the police, we must first open the lines of communication within our own households and bring up topics that perhaps make us feel uncomfortable, like the conversation I had with my youngest daughter, who during the Seattle protests in 2020 told me: "If you are part of the police force, you are part of the problem." As a young Black woman who was demonstrating against police brutality, she felt strongly about supporting the Black

Lives Matter movement—which I agreed with—but struggled with having her mother being the police chief.

So, as uncomfortable as it might have been, we sat down and had that conversation, the one where we try to come to terms with the dichotomy I represent as a Black woman at the head of the police department. I explained to her the way I saw my role and why I thought it mattered—especially in that moment. She explained to me why she struggled with it. I answered her questions and she listened to what I had to say. And what more could you really ask for? Two generations coming together to discuss issues that have existed in this country for more than four hundred years.

And we must keep that line of communication going, in every American household. Because it was in my own household that, as a child, I learned some of the most important leadership lessons I was able to apply during my career in policing—as well as outside of it.

Our police agencies have to operate with the right people in place because we need to foster a real tie and relationship with our community. We have to develop a sense of fairness and equity. We have to keep talking about it. Because if we keep the conversation going and we invite more and more people to it, we can come to more solutions than the ones I was able to provide. The more we talk about it, the more changes we will be able to implement, and the better things will be.

Race in America used to be an afterthought, one that White America tried hard not to bring up because it made them uncomfortable, or perhaps many thought things were just fine the way they were so there was no need to stir up anything. Now race is at the forefront of every news station, friendly conversation, public debate, academic study, family gathering, and so much more. We are finally facing the elephant in the room. We have come to the point where we have been able to recognize its presence. But now we must all come together to ensure the elephant stops doing so much damage to our homes, our communities, our nation. And, as the American people, we have a big responsibility to ensure that future generations do not have to face such complex, trying, and threatening situations as we had to.

We must recognize that we all have a big role to play. I did not understand that when I first became an officer. I remember being simply concerned with day-to-day stressors such as mortgage and car payments, grocery shopping, and more. But as I grew in my career and life, I realized that each one of us, including myself, has the right and the responsibility to stand up against what is illegal and immoral. We cannot afford to remain silent. Because if history has taught us anything it is that, through us taking a stand and making our voices heard while working together for a common purpose, we are able to bring change.

To conclude, I will say this again: Leadership does not end when you retire. Leadership is a skill set that cannot be applied just in the workplace. It must be passed down to our new generations. I have been a daughter, a sister, a police officer, and a police chief. But I take my roles as mother and now grandmother as the most important ones of my entire life. I know that I can bring about *real* change in the way I have raised my daughters and in the impact that I make in my grand-child's life. Because remember, to beat racism and sex-ism, to fight against police brutality, to truly become one nation that recognizes just how much Black lives do matter, just how much minority groups matter, we must first and foremost erase racism and sexism within our own households.

I know we will get there, and that's why I am so opti-mistic about the future of our country.

# TACTICAL DEBRIEF

**LEADERSHIP DOES NOT** end the moment we retire or change career paths. It is a skill set that we must carry with us and live by whether we are at work or in the comfort of our own home. Each one of us plays a pivotal role in the betterment of our community and society, and it is crucial that we keep an open line of communication, that we sit down to have those uncomfortable conversations, and that we listen to those whose opinion differs from ours. Communicating is the only way we can work together to create a better tomorrow for our newest generations. So, for our final debrief, I invite you to take a look at your leadership skill set and how you have applied the leadership principles you believe in, in both your professional and private life. I invite you to talk to your family members, friends, colleagues, and fellow community members to find ways to eradicate racism and sexism. I invite you to take a seat at the table and join in the conversation by debating and offering suggestions. And finally, I invite you to invite others to join in. Because we need everybody to join in. After all, we are one nation.

# NOTES

## Chapter Three

1. Erin Duffin, "Gender Distribution of Full-Time Law Enforcement Employees in the United States in 2019," Statista, October 1, 2020. https://www.statista .com/statistics/195324/gender-distribution-of-full -time-law-enforcement-employees-in-the-us/.
2. Nikkita Oliver (May 25, 2018), @NikkitaOliver.

## Chapter Four

1. "My Response to The Guardian," Seattle Police Department Blotter, March 10, 2020. https://spd blotter.seattle.gov/2020/03/10/my-response-to -the-guardian/.
2. "Chief Best's Statement to Officers Regarding George Floyd," Seattle Police Department Blotter, May 27, 2020. https://spdblotter.seattle.gov/2020 /05/27/chief-bests-statement-to-officers-regarding -george-floyd/.

3. "Chief's Statement on May 30th's Protests Downtown," Seattle Police Department Blotter, May 31, 2020. https://spdblotter.seattle.gov/2020/05/31/chiefs-statement-on-may-30th-protests-downtown/.

## Chapter Five

1. "Chief Best's Address to Officer," Seattle Police Department Blotter, June 11, 2020. https://spdblotter.seattle.gov/2020/06/11/chief-bests-address-to-officers/.
2. "Chief Best's Letter to the Community on Re-Envisioning Public Safety in Seattle," Seattle Police Department Blotter, June 22, 2020. https://spdblotter.seattle.gov/2020/06/23/re-envisioning-community-safety-in-seattle/.

## Chapter Six

1. "Chief's Letter to City Council in Response to Decriminalize Seattle/King County Equity Now Proposals," Seattle Police Department Blotter, July 22, 2020. https://spdblotter.seattle.gov/2020/07/22/chiefs-letter-to-city-council-in-response-to-decriminalize-seattle-king-county-equity-now-proposals/.
2. "Letter to the Council," Seattle Police Department Blotter, August 2, 2020. https://spdblotter.seattle.gov/2020/08/02/33410/.

3. "Chief Best's Message to the Seattle Police Department and the Community," Seattle Police Department Blotter, August 11, 2020, https://spdblotter.seattle .gov/2020/08/11/chief-bests-message-to-the-seattle -police-department-and-the-community/.

# ABOUT THE AUTHOR

**CARMEN BEST** worked for the Seattle Police Department for twenty-eight years, beginning as an entry-level patrol officer and eventually becoming the first African American woman to serve as chief of police. As chief, she managed approximately two thousand sworn and civilian employees before retiring in 2020.

Prior to becoming chief of police, she served as deputy chief, overseeing the Patrol Operations, Investigations, and Special Operations bureaus, as well as the Community Outreach Program. Among her many accomplishments as chief of police was her creation of the Collaborative Police Bureau, a segment of the SPD encouraging community partnerships and engagement.

Best and the SPD led the nation in implementing safety protocols and practices for first responders in response to COVID-19. She also facilitated record-breaking diversity hiring and recruitment within the department.

Best has lived in the Pacific Northwest her entire life, outside of her service in the US Army, and has received dozens of awards for her contributions to community engagement, public safety, gender equity, and diversity and inclusion. She has received the Newsmaker of the Year award from the Seattle Black Press, the Vision from the Mountaintop award from Urban Impact for her commitment to justice and community, the Influential Woman of 2020 award from the *Puget Sound Business Journal,* and the FBI National Executive Institute Associates National Law Enforcement Ethics Award in 2020. She was awarded the prestigious Ellis Island Medal of Honor, dedicated to recognizing individuals who selflessly contribute to society and uphold the ideals of America, an award that is read into the Congressional Record. Additionally, Best was nominated for an Emmy Award for her work on the PSA series "Safe in the Sound."

Best serves as the Leadership Council chair for the United Negro College Fund, Seattle. She is a board member for United Way of King County, a member of the St. Jude Advisory Council for Seattle and the Seattle University Criminal Justice Advisory Committee, and the cochair of the Human and Civil Rights Committee for the International Association of Chiefs of Police. She is a former member of the IACP Board of Directors and cochair of the Law Enforcement Immigration Task Force. Most recently, she joined the Board of Directors for the Young Women's Christian Council (YWCA) of King County with a mission toward diversity and equity.

Her reach is both local and national as a contributor to MSNBC, CNBC, and NBC News affiliates, and as a law enforcement analyst for KING 5 News in Seattle. She is regularly requested as a subject matter expert and keynote speaker, both locally and nationally, on a variety of topics: leadership, reimagining policing, police reform, race, women in policing, and diversity and inclusion.

Best has a master of science in criminal justice from Northeastern University. She has graduated from the FBI National Executive Institute, the FBI National Academy, the Criminal Justice Executive Leadership Academy, the Major Cities Chiefs Association's Police Executive Leadership Institute, and the Senior Management Institute for Police.

She is a member of the National Organization of Black Law Enforcement Executives and the National Latino Police Officers Association, and is the mother of two adult daughters. Best enjoys hiking in her spare time.